The Vikings

The Vikings

James Graham-Campbell and Dafydd Kidd

The British Museum, London
The Metropolitan Museum of Art, New York

Distributed by
William Morrow and Company, Inc.
New York
1980

First published in Great Britain in 1980 by British
Museum Publications Ltd.

Library of Congress Cataloging in Publication Data

Graham-Campbell, James.
   The Vikings.

   Catalog of an exhibition held at the British Museum,
London, and The Metropolitan Museum of Art, New York.
   Bibliography: p. 200
   Includes index.
   1. Northmen – Exhibitions. I. Kidd, Dafydd, joint
author. II. British Museum. III. New York (City).
Metropolitan Museum of Art.
   IV. Title.
DL65.G64 948′.02′07402142 79–25486
ISBN 0–688–03603–1 (William Morrow and Company, Inc.)
ISBN 0–87099–219–8 (Metropolitan Museum of Art)
ISBN 0–87099–220–1 pbk. (Metropolitan Museum of Art)

Designed by Patrick Yapp

Printed in Great Britain by
Jarrold and Sons Ltd, Norwich

FRONT COVER: *Terminal of a horse-collar from
Mammen, Jutland (28, 89), adapted.*

BACK COVER: *Pendant from Gotland with gold
filigree ornament (54).*

Contents

Photographic Acknowledgments

The majority of the colour photographs have been taken specially for the book by Lennart Larsen of the Danish National Museum in Copenhagen, with a generous grant from the Charles Ulrich and Josephine Bay Foundation given through The Metropolitan Museum of Art, New York. These photographs are the copyright of British Museum Publications Limited; they are listed in italic type under the institution involved, whom we thank for their co-operation in allowing the photographs to be taken. All other photographs are reproduced by kind permission of the following institutions and individuals:

Ålborg Historical Museum: 50, *103*; B. Ambrosiani, Stockholm: 17; Århus University Prehistoric Museum, Moesgård: 46; T. Balslev, Hjørring: 69; Bergen University Historical Museum: *10, 16, 36, 41*; Copenhagen, The National Museum of Denmark; First Department: *14, 28, 44 right, 57, 58, 59, 60, 82, 89, 95b*; Second Department: *12*, 96; P. Dehlholm, Moesgård: 32; Douglas, The Manx Museum and National Trust: 49; Dublin, National Museum of Ireland: 39, 86; Edinburgh, National Museum of Antiquities of Scotland: 7a, 13, 94; Werner Forman Archive, London: 115; Grønlund Forlag, Copenhagen: 70; Lincoln Archaeological Trust: 106 above; London, The British Museum: 1, 2, 63a–b, 67, 68b–l, 81, 106 below, 107; London, The Museum of London: 101; Lund, Kulturen: *22, 27, 34, 51, 72, 75, 79*; Lund, University Historical Museum: *7b*; Oslo University Museum of National Antiquities: *6, 9, 11, 26, 52, 62,* 63c, *71, 73, 90, 92, 95a, 99*; Oslo University Collection of Coins and Medals: 68m; Axel Poignant, London: 30; Reykjavík, The National Museum of Iceland: 38, 45, 113, 114; Rudkøbing, Langeland Museum: 66; Schleswig, Schleswig-Holstein Landesmuseum: *74, 79, 83, 84*; Scandinavian Airlines SAS: 3 (Boberg), 29 (Brorson), 4–5 (Peterson); Stockholm, The National Antiquities Museum: *8, 15a–b, 18, 19, 20, 21, 23, 24, 35, 42, 43, 44, 47, 48, 54, 55, 56, 61, 64, 79, 80, 85, 87, 88, 91, 93, 100, 102, 108, 109, 110, 111*; 40, 98: courtesy of the Antiquities and Topographical Archive, Stockholm; Stockholm, Royal Coin Cabinet, National Museum of Monetary History: 68a; Trondheim Museum: *25, 53, 76, 78, 97, 104, 112*; York Archaeological Trust (M. S. Duffy): 31, 65, 77; Mats Wibe Lund, Reykjavík: 33; D. M. Wilson & O. Klindt-Jensen: 105; Uppsala Museum for Nordic Antiquities: *37*.

The maps for the book were drawn by Eugene Fleury, and the diagrams and illustrations by Jeremy Ford. Figure 4 was redrawn after K. Schietzel, fig. 5 after M. Stenberger, fig. 8 after E. Roesdahl.

Preface

The Vikings have had a bad press. Their activities are equated with rape and pillage and their reputation for brutality is second only to that of the Huns and the Goths. Curiously, they have also been invested with a strange glamour which contradicts in many ways their fearsome image. The wanton, healthy, cheerful, blond Viking has been a firmly established literary figure since the early nineteenth century. The British Museum by means of this book and the exhibition which it illustrates is trying in some ways to redress the balance. In a brutal age the Vikings were brutal, but their brutality was no worse than that of their contemporaries. It is not without significance that the English word *law* has a Scandinavian root, nor that some of the administrative divisions of England in use until the middle of this century were established by Scandinavian settlers. The Vikings were administrators as well as pirates, merchants as well as robbers.

The Scandinavians of the Viking Age had a strong and vital culture of their own, although they were always ready to take up outside influences and ideas. The culture of these people is indicated in this book, as is their daring and adventurous spirit. The discovery of America, the acceptance of Christianity, the creation of nation-states and the government of colonies are all part of this story, as are a distinctive art and considerable technical skill. It is to show all these facets of the Viking character that we have mounted this exhibition and written this book.

It is unlikely that such an exhibition will ever be mounted again and the British Museum's thanks are primarily due to the many museums in different countries, both within Scandinavia and elsewhere, for lending so many national treasures (the numerous lending institutions are listed below). The sponsorship of Times Newspapers Ltd in association with Scandinavian Airlines System must be acknowledged with gratitude; in particular the names of Asbjörn Engen, Vice President at SAS Head Office, Steen Larsen, General Manager SAS Great Britain and Ireland, and Derek Jewell, Publishing Director Times Newspapers Ltd, deserve a special mention. The generosity of SAS has been demonstrated in most practical terms by the transport of material and people between Norway, Sweden and Denmark and London. Priceless Viking objects – national treasures of their countries – have been brought to the British Museum with infinite care. A major grant from the Cultural Fund of the Nordic Council has immeasurably helped the exhibition organisers. It would be invidious to name too many individuals but without the help and active support of Sir Denis Hamilton, Kenneth Pearson, Ralph Cohen and James Graham-Campbell this exhibition would not have been possible.

Further the co-operation of the Arhus Prehistoric Museum at Moesgård (and particularly the help of Professor Ole Klindt-Jensen and Holger Schmidt) in the reconstruction of a house from the Viking town of Hedeby must be acknowledged with grateful thanks. In private duty bound I must also thank two members of the British Museum staff, Dafydd Kidd and Jean Rankine, for the energy which they have devoted to the preparation of this exhibition.

This is the first time that the British Museum has arranged an exhibition together with The Metropolitan Museum of Art, New York (where it will be shown in the autumn), and we trust that the happy co-operation experienced in this project will extend far into the future.

David M. Wilson
DIRECTOR
THE BRITISH MUSEUM

The authors wish to thank Mr H. Johannsen of the SAS London office and Mrs E. Thorvildsen of the Danish National Museum First Department for their good offices; Miss M. Archibald, F.S.A., of the British Museum Department of Coins and Medals for her selection of coins for illustration, and checking of the related text; Mrs G. Boyce and Mrs L. Leth-Larsen for their help in preparation of this catalogue and Mrs V. Bottomley and Miss V. Springett for their typing; Miss S. Beeby for her help.

List of Lenders

Ålborg Historical Museum
Andreas Church, Isle of Man
The Antiquities Museum, Ribe
Århus University Prehistoric Museum, Moesgård
Bangsbo Museum, Fredrikshavn
Bergen University Historical Museum
Boher Church and the Bishop of Ardagh and Clonmacnoise
British Museum, Departments of Coins and Medals,
    and Medieval and Later Antiquities
Canterbury City Museum
The Dean and Chapter Library, Durham
The Department of the Environment, London
Gävle Museum
Goldsborough Rectory, Yorkshire
Ipswich Museum
Kulturen (Culture History Museum), Lund
Langeland Museum, Rudkøbing
Lincoln Archaeological Trust
Lincolnshire Museums
Lund University Historical Museum
Manx Museum and National Trust, Douglas
Middleton Church, Pickering, Yorkshire
Museum for Nordic Antiquities, Uppsala
Museum of London
National Board of Antiquities and Historical Monuments, Helsinki
National Antiquities Museum, Stockholm
National Maritime History Museum, Stockholm
National Museum of Antiquities of Scotland, Edinburgh
National Museum of Denmark, Copenhagen
National Museum of Iceland, Reykjavik
National Museum of Ireland, Dublin
Oslo University Collection of Coins and Medals
Oslo University Museum of National Antiquities
Royal Coin Cabinet, National Museum of Monetary History, Stockholm
Royal Norwegian Scientific Society Museum, Trondheim
Saffron Walden Museum
Schleswig-Holstein Landesmuseum, Schleswig
Sigtuna Kommun Museums
Sydhimmerlands Museum, Hobro
Tromsø Museum
Viking Ship Museum, Roskilde
Winchester Research Unit and the Dean and Chapter, Winchester
Wisbech and Fenland Museum
York District Council through the York Archaeological Trust
York Minster Museum
The Yorkshire Museum, York

1 Introduction and the Scandinavian Background

In the year AD 789 the Wessex king's representative, Beaduheard, hurried with a band of men from the town of Dorchester to Portland on the southern English coast. He was to investigate three ships thought to be traders. Their crews murdered him and his companions. 'And those', records the Anglo-Saxon Chronicle dryly, and with over a century of grim hindsight, 'were the first ships of the Danish men which came to the land of the English.' In 793 'ravages of heathen men miserably destroyed God's church on Lindisfarne with plunder and slaughter'. The Christian monastic sites of Jarrow and Iona lying on Britain's exposed northern coasts were looted in the years immediately after. In 795 raiders were recorded near Dublin, and in 799 on the coast of south-west France. As far as we know this was all the work of Norwegians. The first raids by Danes in the west were on Frisia and in 834 the thriving and populous trading centre of Dorestad on the Rhine Estuary was attacked.

This was the beginning of a period of history known to us as the Viking Age, when Scandinavian peoples from the modern countries of Norway, Sweden and Denmark dominated much of northern Europe and beyond. They travelled further than Europeans had ever done before and established regular communications over great distances. They exploited the riches of the eastern world and explored the uncharted waters of the North Atlantic Ocean. They settled as farmers in the barren western lands of Greenland and discovered America; they served as mercenaries at the court of Byzantium. They ravaged and destroyed Christian Anglo-Saxon kingdoms, and the Carolingian Empire was penetrated to its heart. They extorted massive blackmail of silver and gold. Yet they also went on to colonise rich commercial centres from York to Kiev, and formed powerful states.

It was an age when wealth rapidly changed hands; Scandinavians without silver sought to acquire it by whatever means, and gain power and prestige by redistributing it. The great Viking silver hoard of coins, ingots and cut-up jewellery from Cuerdale in Lancashire, hidden in the early tenth century, illustrates the ambitions and uncertainties of the period (1).

From the eighth to eleventh centuries Scandinavian groups developed from being unorganised raiders and powerful predatory armies into aggressive national states professing the Christian faith. Their adversaries, and victims, developed their own political and military organisation for defence. When peace and stability again returned, the explosion of population from Scandinavia had permanently altered the map of northern Europe and its power structure. National kingdoms had formed in Scandinavia from about AD 1000, while Viking communities outside

1 *Silver hoard from Cuerdale, Lancashire, hidden at the beginning of the tenth century.*

THE WEST	SCANDINAVIA AND THE CONTINENT	THE EAST

THE WEST

- late 8th century — Norwegians settling Orkney and Shetland
- 789 — Viking ships off S. England
- 793–5 — Lindisfarne, Jarrow and Iona sacked
- 795 — Vikings raid near Dublin
- 830s — Raids on Ireland intensify
- 835 — Beginning of 30 years' attacks on England by Viking armies
- 840s — Dublin established as Viking base
- 851 — Danish army first winters in England
- c. 860 — Scandinavian discovery of Iceland
- 865 — First 'Danegeld' from England
- 867 — York taken by Vikings
- 871–99 — Alfred 'the Great' king of Wessex
- 876 — Vikings divide up Northumbria
- 878 — King Alfred defeats Guthrum
- 886 — Treaty partitions England Scandinavians settle Danelaw
- 910–18 — Beginning reconquest of Danelaw by Anglo-Saxons
- 930 — Icelandic republic established
- 954 — Eirík 'Bloodaxe' of York killed England unified
- 980 — Battle of Tara reduces power of Viking kings of Dublin
- 980s — Renewal of systematic Danish raids on England
- 986 — Eirík 'the Red' settles Greenland
- 985/6 — First Scandinavians sight America
- 999 — Iceland adopts Christianity
- 1002 — Danes massacred on St Brice's Day in S. England
- 1017–35 — Knut 'the Great' rules Anglo-Scandinavian Kingdom
- 1051 — Scandinavian mercenaries paid off by English
- 1066 — English defeat Norwegians at Stamford Bridge; English defeated at Hastings
- 1069/70 — Sven Estridsson of Denmark invades England but makes peace
- 1085 — Knut 'the Holy' fails to reconquer England

SCANDINAVIA AND THE CONTINENT

- late 8th century — Ribe and Paviken flourish; Cufic coins from Muslim world reaching E. Scandinavia
- 799 — S. W. France attacked by Vikings
- 808 — Godfred destroys Slav town of Reric and settles Hedeby
- 810 — Godfred ravages Frisian coast
- 815 — Denmark invaded by Empire
- 829 — Ansgar's first Scandinavian mission
- 834 — Danes plunder town of Dorestad
- 845 — Vikings burn Hamburg, ravage Paris and Spanish towns
- 849 — Ansgar's second mission
- 850 — First church built at Hedeby
- 860s — Vikings raid N. Africa and Italy
- 870 — Monk Rimbert writes life of Ansgar
- 885 — Paris besieged by Vikings
- early 10th century — Decline of Kaupang
- 911 — Vikings granted Normandy
- 934 — Germans capture Hedeby
- 935 — New mission to the Danes
- c. 965 — Conversion of Harald 'Bluetooth' king of Denmark
- 970s — Decline of Birka and rise of Sigtuna
- 974 — German Otto II seizes Hedeby
- c. 994 — Olaf Tryggvason king of Norway converted
- 990s — Bergen and Trondheim founded
- 1008 — Olaf Sköttkonung king of Sweden converted
- c. 1020 — Lund founded
- 1030 — Olaf Haraldsson (St Olaf) king of Norway killed
- 1064 — Treaty separates Denmark and Norway
- 1066 — Hedeby sacked by Slavs; Superseded by Schleswig
- 1075–80 — Adam of Bremen writes his history

THE EAST

- 839 — Reference to Swedes in Byzantium
- 860s — Traditional dates for first Viking activity in Russia; Rus attack Byzantium
- 874 — Commercial treaty between Byzantines and Rus who accept bishop
- 882 — Viking Oleg traditionally takes over Kiev
- 907 — Rus attack on Byzantium
- 912 — Vikings attack Baku on Caspian
- 921/2 — Ibn Fadlan describes Rus on Volga
- 950 — Emperor Constantine writes about Rus
- c. 965 — Sviatoslav of Kiev attacks Bolgars
- Volga eastern trade disrupted
- 972 — Vladimir siezes power in Novgorod
- c. 1000 — Varangian Guard at Byzantium
- 1015–54 — Jaroslav 'the Wise' king in Kiev

Scandinavia were gradually subjected to local control. This slow process ended at different times in different areas, lastly in the west. England was firmly removed from the Scandinavian political orbit by Norman kings after 1066. Iceland had become officially Christian from AD 1000, but resisted the imposition of direct Norwegian control until 1262. In Ireland the Battle of Tara in 980 left the Vikings of Dublin with a semi-independent existence which ended with the English conquest from 1169.

To their western adversaries these Scandinavians were known simply as 'Northmen', or more specifically from their country or district of origin. The Arabs referred to them as 'fire-worshippers', or 'heathens'. To the Byzantines they were sometimes simply 'barbarians'. But now the term 'Viking' has gained universal currency, synonymous with piracy, rapine

2 ABOVE *The Vikings as they may have appeared to their victims: an Anglo-Saxon stone from Lindisfarne, Northumberland.*

Fig. 1 OPPOSITE *An outline of some principal events in Viking history.*

and cruelty. The derivation of the name is uncertain: it has been linked to trading journeys, seafaring or dwelling in creeks and bays – all activities based on the sea. And to go 'a-Viking' meant joining an expedition across the sea to gain riches and honour. Much of our contemporary written information about the Vikings comes from their victims. In western Europe the activities of Norwegians and Danes were recorded by cloistered, monkish chroniclers bewailing attacks on religious houses or on Christian armies. Their dry, laconic lists of disaster after disaster contrast with rhetorical outbursts. A twelfth-century Irish saga describes these 'ruthless, wrathful, foreign, purely pagan people'.

The unexpected and sudden nature of the early raids gave them an air of mystery and the supernatural. A stone sculpture from Lindisfarne, perhaps recalling the disaster of its sack in 793, shows one view of the Vikings (2). The success of the Viking hit-and-run tactics gave rise to reports of exaggerated numbers of men and ships. The extent of the

Lapps

HÁLOGALAND

Gulf of Bothnia

NORRLAND

Finns

□ Lade
Trondheim

Gulf of Finland

DALARNA

Åland Islands

Bergen

UPPLAND
Valsgärde
Old Uppsala ● ▲ □ *Sigtuna*
Birka ■
Helgö ●

Borre ▲
Oseberg ▲
Gokstad ▲ ▲ Tune
Kaupang ■

□ *Skara*

GOTLAND
● Paviken

Lindholm Høje
Aggersborg ◉ **ÖLAND**
Alborg **HALLAND**
Limfjord □
Viborg ◉ Fyrkat **BLEKINGE**
▲ Mammen **SKÅNE**
□ *Århus*
JUTLAND Lejre ● **BALTIC
SEA**
Jelling ▲
Ribe ■ □ *Lund*
◉ Trelleborg

NORTH SEA

Balts

Hedeby

○ Ringforts
▲ Burials
■ Early towns
□ Late towns
● Other sites
······ Borders of the Danish Kingdom
– – – Hærvej

Germans   Slavs

destruction they perpetrated was calculated to terrorise, but the stories told may not all be true history.

Sophisticated Arabs encountered the Scandinavians trading down the great Russian rivers through eastern Slav territory, and eastern merchants visited the principal trade-centres of Scandinavia. To them the Vikings appeared rude and coarse and dangerous, interesting as ethnographical curiosities. 'They are the dirtiest of God's creatures . . . and they do not wash themselves after sex . . .' wrote the fastidious Ibn Fadlan in the early tenth century of a group of northern merchants.

Viking raids south across the Caspian Sea in the tenth century were repulsed; western attacks on the Mediterranean Arab emirates of North Africa and Spain were only moderately successful. It was largely in exchange for fur and slaves that the Vikings obtained masses of silver from the Arabs. In the east the Vikings appear as vagabonds of dubious reputation. In conjunction with Slav forces from Kiev they sometimes mounted sporadic sea-borne attacks in the tenth century to extort commercial concessions from Byzantium, but were no serious danger except when their attacks coincided with those from other quarters. The Arabs and Byzantines were technically superior to the Vikings, whose power was weak at such distances, and since they were politically more centralised and united than western states they could defend themselves successfully. It was the weakness of political control and the fragmentation of western Europe which allowed the Vikings such easy success in their early raids. But whenever there was a way out of a stern fight the Vikings found it. They were more concerned with profit than empty glory.

From the Icelandic sagas recorded three centuries later than the events described, we gain a view of the Vikings as men of a heroic age. The sagas are a Nordic tradition, a reflection of the medieval literature of romance, composed to entertain rather than as history. Against a background of anonymous common people, striking characters appear, larger than life, with comic foibles and exaggerated virtues and vices.

It has been the fate of the Vikings to be seen in an idealised or unrealistic light. A single facet of their character or activities has too often been isolated to make the moral or political point that they were savage, destructive barbarians or – much later – a blue-eyed, fair-haired Aryan master race. In reality there was never one Viking people. During this period a northern version of the Germanic language was commonly understood across Scandinavia, which enabled groups from different areas to co-operate on joint enterprises. But within Scandinavia itself landscape and environment imposed differences on the inhabitants, and their political allegiances varied.

The home of the Vikings, Scandinavia, consisted of the three present-day kingdoms of Denmark, Sweden and Norway, and part of Finland. Their combined land mass is huge, extending over twelve hundred miles from north to south: northern Norway extends well inside the Arctic Circle, and the original border of the Danish Viking kingdom was at the base of the Jutland Peninsula in what is today northern Germany. Massive erosion of some areas by Ice-Age glaciers, and deposition in others of

Fig. 2 Viking-Age Scandinavia.

varied materials during glacial retreats, has produced lands of great contrasts.

In the south is a geographical unit consisting of the Jutland Peninsula, the five hundred or so Danish islands, and the rich provinces of southern Sweden: Skåne, Halland and Blekinge. Here the land is comparatively flat, and the soils relatively light and fertile. The area is an extension of the North European Plain and is linked to it only by a narrow land bridge at the base of the Jutland Peninsula. The importance of Danish towns such as Hedeby derives from the exploitation of the overland and river route across this neck between the North Sea and the Baltic. A narrow sea-opening between Jutland and west Sweden controls the strategic but dangerous entrance into the Baltic around the top of the Jutland Peninsula from the North Sea. Apart from areas of bog, forest and desolate sandy heathland the area is agriculturally rich. Transport is relatively easy, and expanses of sea or deep penetrating rivers are links in communication rather than barriers. The sea dominates the land, being never far distant. Much of this south-west Baltic area formed an early political unit, the kingdom of Denmark, because of its relative uniformity and over-all accessibility.

To the north-east of the Danish kingdom, separated by dense forests and lakes, lie the provinces of Sweden. Much of this area is covered by waterways, with lakes and bogs and forests. Areas of rich and poor agricultural land are mixed up. Inland waters and ridges providing land routes made Uppland in east-central Sweden a natural centre for early settlement. Its deep and protected inland waterway system gave Uppland access to the extensive Swedish coast and the rich Baltic islands of Öland and Gotland, and accounts for the importance of the sites Helgö, Birka and Sigtuna. To the north were sparsely settled areas of agricultural land amid forests and lakes, and along the coast of the Gulf of Bothnia there were settlements around river mouths. The strategic position of Gotland in the centre of the Baltic, with its rich limestone-based soils, made it a naturally independent centre.

A long inhospitable mountain spine separates Sweden from Norway. Routes across this barrier were few, giving prominence to areas either side of the passes. One of these linked Trøndelag, the west-coast area around Trondheim, eastwards to the head of the Gulf of Bothnia and so to the Baltic. Rich lowlands form an irregular fringe around the Norwegian coast, penetrating deep inland along the fjord valleys, a stark contrast to the barren uplands which form the mass of the landscape. The very long, indented coastline is protected by lines of offshore islands. Natural land barriers and the scattering of population over long distances make sea transport essential. The warm Gulf Stream prevents the northern seas from freezing and affects local temperature well above the Arctic Circle, making Norway habitable at very high latitudes. Sea access around the North Cape to the White Sea is also possible. Main natural centres are

3 LEFT *A northern Swedish landscape: forests and lakes in Ångermanland.*
4 OVERLEAF *A Norwegian landscape: the Geiranger Fjord, penetrating deep inland.*

situated in the lowland plains of the south and south-west. Around the Oslo Fjord in the south are a series of rich ship-burials and the town of Kaupang. Much of the political history of Norway lies in its resistance to interference from Denmark, and the imposing of control from the south on the northern communities scattered along the coast and inland. In the north the Earldom of Lade was a minor centre.

Scandinavian geography is dominated by the sea and inland waterways and the possibilities they offer for communication. Because of the contrast between rich and poor agricultural land, affected by relief and drainage, there are formed natural areas for settlement. Barriers to communication – forests, bogs and mountains – dictate the relationships between those communities.

Scandinavia was inhabited by farmers where the land was productive. Farms were often single units worked by family groups, clustering more densely where the land was best. Farming was supplemented by hunting and fishing where possible. Larger concentrations of people, who gained their living by trade and commerce, sometimes protected by small hill-forts, had only rarely appeared in Scandinavia by the beginning of the Viking Age. In the next centuries their number and size increased. Villages began to be organised in some areas only at the end of the period. Control of land, that is family wealth, was of paramount importance. Many sons in a landowning family made it powerful, since the dowries brought by their wives enabled the family to extend and consolidate its territory. The family could, in a legal sense and for recognising obligations, be defined up to the degree of third or fourth cousins, recognising a common great-, great-, great-grandfather. The bond between a territorial chief, his followers and their families was also a strong and pervasive one, often ending only in death. We know very little about the details of pre-Viking social systems which bound everyone. The history of the Viking period is one of rapid change in social relationships and the introduction of new economic forces.

Some Scandinavians attempted to improve their position by leaving their homeland to gain wealth in the territories around Scandinavia, and returned with their status increased. Although many went a-Viking, the majority stayed at home, trying to profit from the changing situation. But the idea that the Vikings suddenly emerged as a phenomenon peculiar to the ninth, tenth and eleventh centuries is a misconception based on their sudden explosion into the consciousness of western Europe. Their unheralded appearance in the written records of Christian chroniclers belies centuries of steady internal development and foreign contact that preceded the Viking Age.

During the last centuries before the birth of Christ weapons, tools and agricultural implements began to be made from iron, a local raw material, making Scandinavia independent of imported bronze except for making jewellery. Climatic changes resulting in warmer, drier conditions made agriculture more productive. Population gradually increased, becoming richer and more stratified. From the first to early fifth centuries AD the Roman Empire established frontiers in the west, incorporating the rivers

Rhine and Danube. Scandinavia never became part of the Empire. In consequence it never had imposed on it the towns, bureaucracy and latterly Christianity, which were features common to all the Roman provinces and which strongly influenced their later development.

Groups of Scandinavians migrated across to the south Baltic coast and deeper inland: the Goths, for instance, moved from the Baltic in the second century AD and by the fourth century had established a kingdom in the Ukraine and south Russia. Some tribes in the Elbe Valley claimed Scandinavian origins. One sixth-century author had no doubt as to Scandinavia's rôle, referring to the area as 'the birthplace of tribes'. A large-scale, long-distance trade between the provinces of the Empire and areas outside grew up. The wealth and social prestige of rich farmers and chieftains in Scandinavia were expressed by possession of luxury Roman exports: glass vessels, bronze drinking equipment (especially associated with imported wine), bronze and silver tableware, jewellery, specially made weapons (particularly swords) and rich cloths. Imported gold and silver were melted down and made into prestige jewellery.

In return we may suppose a range of foodstuffs, leather for army supplies, and luxuries such as furs, amber and slaves were traded southwards. Some goods travelled direct by water transport: the Rhine and north German coast route and rivers flowing into the Baltic were heavily used. Other goods changed hands many times. Sites such as Dankirke at the base of the Jutland Peninsula and Helgö in Uppland became prominent trading centres. Areas such as Fyn, Sjælland and Gotland in the Baltic were important in controlling traffic. In the third and fourth centuries particularly, long-distance trade appears to have stimulated local trade and craft specialisation.

In the later fourth century began a series of westward moves by Germanic tribes resulting in the collapse of the Western Empire in the fifth century and the establishment of small kingdoms by the invaders. Large areas of north-west Germany, and the territory of the Angles in south-east Jutland and the Jutes in south-west Jutland, were abandoned from the mid fifth century. These peoples migrated along the Frisian coast to Britain.

During the fifth and sixth centuries in central and eastern Europe a wave of migrations by peasant Slavs occurred. Soon they occupied the south Baltic coast from Holstein in north Germany to the River Vistula in east Poland, extending southward as far as the Adriatic Sea. During the fifth and early sixth centuries a mass of gold coin flooded into east Scandinavia from the eastern Mediterranean Byzantine Empire, perhaps by way of the south-east Baltic coast and the Polish and west Russian river systems. Slav movements and the westward advance of the nomadic Avars from the steppe appear to have interrupted this contact in the early sixth century. During this period of migrations there appears to have been widespread piracy and warfare in the west Baltic. From the later fourth century there had been large-scale deposits of sacrificed weapons in southern Scandinavian bogs; farms were burnt out and deserted; settlements retreated from some exposed coasts and were defended, while others lay

5 *The Åland archipelago between Sweden and Finland.*

near local fortified refuges. In the fifth and sixth centuries particularly, hoards of precious metals were deposited but never recovered. Imported gold coin and silver looted from Roman provinces circulating in hoards of cut-up fragments were reused in jewellery and other ornaments.

From the fifth century, there emerged over the Germanic world groups of powerful men who were distinguished by burial with rich weapons, gold or silver jewellery, and imported luxuries. The richest is the burial in a ship of an early seventh-century East Anglian king, at Sutton Hoo in Suffolk. Its best parallels are found in Uppland in east-central Sweden; the East Anglian royal dynasty claimed Swedish antecedents.

In the seventh and eighth centuries there was a period of political consolidation and relative peace in northern Europe. In England lay a group of Germanic kingdoms; to the west, north and in Ireland, were Celtic kingdoms, and in north and east Scotland the Picts. The Frankish kings had united modern France and western Germany by conquests, and their successors, the Carolingian dynasty, pursued an aggressive eastern policy against Slavs and Avars. Their conquests along the North Sea coast brought them into contact with the Danes, and they shared a frontier at the base of the Jutland Peninsula. Along the south Baltic coast Slav tribes were consolidating into leagues and more centralised political units. The Balts on the south-east coast were organised into tribal units, while the Finns formed an even looser political group along the north-east coast and along the Gulf of Finland.

Stability encouraged an increasing volume of trade in Europe. In the west there developed a series of undefended market and trade centres, and regular traffic routes, especially on the coasts of the English Channel and around the North Sea.

Some Scandinavian centres such as Ribe and Helgö (the predecessor of Birka) were active before the Viking period. More important centres in the west which the Vikings raided – London, York, Quentovic and Dorestad – and others on the south Baltic coast were also of importance before the Viking Age. Trade contacts with Scandinavia during this period are reflected in scattered groups of rich material in burials and trading sites. In the east, Swedes from Uppland and Gotland had already begun to settle on the east Baltic coast during the seventh century and to explore further afield. The literature is silent about these early-developed relationships, and only archaeology can reveal the truth.

Thus during the eighth century Scandinavia was at the centre of an arc of politically developing, economically active peoples to the west and south, while immediately to the east lay poorer, rather less organised groups. It was the sea which was the common link.

2 Ships and the Sea

'Never before has such a terror appeared in Britain as we have now suffered from a pagan race, nor was it thought that such an inroad from the sea could be made.' So commented Alcuin in 793 when he heard of the Viking raid on Lindisfarne. What at first amazed the English was the speed of the Vikings' operations. Their ships appeared out of nowhere and ran in through the surf on to the beach, so that warriors could leap straight into action – and then they departed again as quickly as they had come. Though such feats were not thought possible in western Europe in the late eighth century, it was soon widely discovered to be otherwise.

For Viking shipbuilders had perfected reliable sailing-ships that had no need of deep water, safe anchorages or quaysides. Their construction and shallow draught allowed them to use any sloping beach as their harbour and to manœuvre in waters unsuitable for most European vessels of that time. No wonder that surprise was felt, along with terror and rage, at such raids, for it was not just islands, like Lindisfarne, or coastal settlements that suffered at the hands of the Vikings. They rowed their ships up rivers that led them to rich inland cities and monasteries – up the Thames and the Shannon, the Elbe and the Seine, the Loire and the Rhône, and many, many more. That the Viking Age in western Europe began when it did must be attributed largely to the development of such ships in Scandinavia during the eighth century.

The Scandinavian tradition of shipbuilding during the Viking Age was characterised by slender and flexible boats, with symmetrical ends and a true keel; they were clinker-built – that is of overlapping planks riveted together. There is as yet no archaeological evidence to show how and when Scandinavian ships evolved for use with a sail, for the earliest known Viking ships – such as that found in the great Norwegian ship-burial at Oseberg – are already fully adapted for sailing. But there are pictures of sailing-ships on stones, on the Baltic island of Gotland, that have been dated to the seventh century.

In the summer of 1880 a large mound was opened at Gokstad, on the west side of the Oslo Fjord, and was found to contain the well-preserved (if somewhat flattened) remains of a ship. A burial-chamber had been erected aft to house the body of a six-foot Viking, aged about fifty. His grave had been so richly furnished that it had proved all too tempting to grave-robbers; the chamber had been emptied of his weapons and most other personal goods. But also in the burial were at least twelve horses and six dogs, not forgetting his peacock – a most exotic import. There was a range of household goods and kitchen equipment, including a large cauldron that would have sufficed for cooking the crew's dinner when they camped

6 *The Gokstad ship: fine lines and massive keel attest its speed and strength.*

25

ashore for the night. His own tent-posts were included, along with six beds, and also alternative forms of transport, consisting of a sledge and three small rowing-boats. These graceful craft are still unique survivals a hundred years after their discovery and serve to fill out the lines of similar small boats used in lesser ship-burials. All three were made of oak; two had two pairs of oars and the other had three. They were steered with a side-rudder fitted to the starboard side, like the big ship itself. Experiments with a modern replica of one of them have fully demonstrated their functional qualities, and replicas of the large ship (and others found since) have been equally successful. The first of these was built in 1893 and sailed across the Atlantic in the year of Columbus's quatercentenary.

The Gokstad ship was removed from its bed of blue clay, which had been its protection in the ground, and can now be seen, reconstructed, in the Viking Ship Museum in Oslo (6). Apart from the mast and the decking (made of pine), most of the ship was built of oak with the keel consisting of a single timber, nearly 58 feet long. The over-all length is $76\frac{1}{2}$ feet, with a width of $17\frac{1}{2}$ feet amidships, but even when fully laden it would have drawn only 3 feet of water. The clinker-built hull was lashed to the ribs with roots of spruce to ensure the vessel's flexibility. The mast was seated in a massive block of timber, attached to the keel, and could be raised or lowered as required. When raised such masts were generally supported by a forestay and a pair of shrouds, as sketched by a Viking artist on a stone from Jarlshof in Shetland (7a). The single rectangular sail was hoisted on a yard; the one on the Gokstad ship was nearly 40 feet long. Such a sail can be seen lowered and furled in the sketch on the whetstone found at Löddeköppinge (7b), or raised and in use on the Smiss stone from Gotland (8). These pictures also illustrate the use of a side-rudder, as

7a BELOW *The simple outlines of a ship scratched on stone by a Viking on Shetland.*

7b BELOW RIGHT *The sail is lowered, but still the helmsman stands to his rudder in this sketch from southern Sweden.*

found on all Viking ships. This was a device of great efficiency, much praised by Magnus Andersen who captained the Atlantic crossing of the 1893 replica.

When sailing was impossible, the Gokstad ship would have been rowed; there were sixteen oars a side and the oar-holes had hinged discs on the inside to close them when not in use. Since there were no fixed benches, the oarsmen would have had to seat themselves on their own sea-chests. With thirty-two oarsmen, the helmsman and the captain, the crew will have numbered at least thirty-four. The ship was buried with a row of shields along either side, overlapping each other and painted alternately yellow and black. It could not have been rowed with the shields in this position because they blocked the oar-holes, but they could have been so displayed at anchor. The Oseberg ship, discovered in 1904, had a different kind of arrangement. It had a special rack which enabled it to be rowed with the shields on display (so affording some extra protection to the rowers). In the light of recent finds of more specialised vessels, the Gokstad ship must be interpreted as a general-purpose sea-going ship. On the other hand, the ornate Oseberg ship was much less seaworthy and cannot have been used safely in other than sheltered coastal waters.

Its discovery, also in a large mound on the west side of the Oslo Fjord, was one of the most dramatic events in the history of archaeology, for the airtight mound had preserved for a thousand years a wealth of objects that transformed all knowledge of life in the early Viking Age. The unusual choice of a ship for a woman's burial suggests that its main occupant was high-born. The young lady who was buried in a chamber built in the after-part of the ship was accompanied to the grave by her maidservant, for the body of an old and rheumaticky woman was also present. She was

provided with a complete cross-section of items, both large and small, that she had used in life and might have use for again. Grave robbers had stripped the young woman of her finery, and one of the three chests buried with her had been badly broken and emptied of its contents. What was left, however, is amazing for its variety and, in many cases, for the quality of its carved ornament.

The Oseberg lady must have been a keen traveller, for buried with her was an ornate cart, three lavishly carved sledges (with a fourth workaday example), and her saddle. The skeletons of at least ten horses and two oxen were discovered. Then there were the posts for two tents and three beds, together with their bedding and various textiles, including both clothes and ornamental wall-hangings. Five animal-headed posts are masterpieces of the wood-carver's art, but of unknown use. The variety of household goods, kitchen equipment and textile implements can only be appreciated by a visit to the Viking Ship Museum.

Like the Gokstad ship and all other major Viking vessels, the one found at Oseberg is a large, open boat designed for both sailing and rowing. The Oseberg ship is slightly smaller than the Gokstad and was provided with thirty oars; it is altogether of lighter and less robust construction. But most striking is the carved ornament of the bow and stern, with the strongly curving prow ending in a serpent's head, recalling a poet's description of such a ship as a 'snake of the sea'. The most usual poetic epithets, however, concern horses, such as 'sail-horses' or 'sea-steeds'.

Both the Oseberg and Gokstad ships contained numerous movable accessories, from remains of the sails and their rigging, to the ships' iron anchors and their wooden gangplanks. Other important equipment for an open boat were wooden bailers. The T-shaped crutches in the Gokstad ship, which would have held the lowered yard with its furled sail, would also have enabled awnings to be erected in harbour to provide some little shelter. Medieval sagas refer to large skin bags which were used for storage of gear and weapons during the day and which served as two-man sleeping-bags at night. But whenever possible Viking sailors preferred to follow coastal routes, where they could put ashore to cook and sleep each night. On longer Atlantic voyages supplies of dried or salted meat and fish, and of water, sour milk and beer would have to be carried; both ship-burials were provided with casks for this purpose, although water might also have been carried in skins.

All such equipment is missing from the remarkable group of late Viking-Age ships raised from the bed of the Roskilde Fjord at Skuldelev in 1962 (where they had been deliberately stripped and sunk in the early eleventh century to block an approach to the town of Roskilde). The investigation and recovery of these five vessels of widely differing types revolutionised our knowledge of Viking ships and allowed Gokstad and Oseberg to be seen in perspective for the first time.

Firstly, there were the remains of a true Viking 'longship', some ninety-five feet long and built of oak. It appears to have been able to carry a force of fifty to sixty men, but is so far without parallel. Yet larger ships are known from the literary sources, the most famous being the *Long Serpent*,

8 *A ship full of Viking warriors on a Gotlandic stone. (The paint is modern.)*

built by Olaf Tryggvason, near Trondheim, probably in the winter of 998. The story of its building was first recorded about 1200, and we are told that it had thirty-two or thirty-four pairs of oars. Its length would have been perhaps a hundred and twenty feet. Such a ship would have been exceptional and there is unlikely to have been more than one like it in any fleet.

The most important of these ship-finds from Skuldelev are undoubtedly the two cargo-vessels. For the first time it was possible to see the types of ships that the Vikings used for coastal trade and their ventures into deep-sea waters, such as during the colonisation of Iceland. These are both broader and deeper than the ships so far discussed; they also have an open space amidships for stowing the cargo, which means that they only have oar-holes at the prow and stern.

The smallest of the Skuldelev ships is a thirty-nine-foot fishing-boat, or perhaps a ferry. Finally, there is an example of what was the standard type of warship of medium size, capable of carrying twenty-six to thirty men directly on to a beach, in the manner so vividly portrayed in the Bayeux tapestry, which records the Norman invasion of England in 1066. It is a type known also from tenth-century ship-burials at Ladby in Denmark and at Hedeby, but only as shadows in the ground.

Such wrecks and ship-burials tell us little, however, of the external appearance of Viking ships as they gathered in a fjord before setting out on an expedition. From the poets of the eleventh and twelfth centuries we can imagine that it was a colourful scene; one describes the ships, for example, as 'gold-mouthed splendid beasts of the mast, bright painted'. The sails of the ships were coloured and the mast-heads fitted with pennants or vanes, of which some survive from ships of the late Viking Age because they were reused on churches.

The example from Heggen in Norway (9) shows the typical form. Made from heavily gilt bronze, the vane itself is incised with animal and plant patterns (described in Chapter 11), with a proud beast mounted on top to keep watch over the horizon. A series of small holes along the lower edge was for the attachment of streamers, or metal pendants that would have rattled and jangled in the breeze. Such metal vanes were still in use in Scandinavia after the Viking period, as can be seen in a thirteenth-century sketch of a massed fleet on a piece of wood excavated in Bergen, Norway.

Those same ships that struck fear into the hearts of the Vikings' victims must have been a source of excitement and pride to their Scandinavian builders and sailors. But, sophisticated and technically perfect though their ships were, the sea-borne successes of the Vikings depended as much on their skilled seamanship and a great deal of bravery. Their preference for coastal navigation can be quite understood given the lack of amenities on board, but their Atlantic voyages of exploration and settlement would have meant days in open sea without sight of land. There is considerable dispute about the types of navigational equipment possessed by the Vikings; whatever they may have been, they would certainly not have been accurate enough to determine a ship's position while at sea. The sun and the stars would have been observed when natural landmarks were out of

9 Gilded vane for an eleventh-century Viking ship.

sight, as would have the movements of birds and sea mammals. Taken together with a knowledge of wind and current, preserved in memory, such voyages could be made and repeated, even though the hazards remained great. To us the achievements of these Scandinavian boat-builders and navigators are a matter of great wonder and admiration, but to them it was matter of fact. One version of the Icelandic *Landnámabók*, originally compiled in the twelfth century, gives these simple instructions for sailing directly from Norway to Greenland:

> From Hernar in Norway one is to keep sailing west for Hvarf in Greenland and then you will sail north of Shetland so that you can just see it in very clear weather; but south of the Faeroes so that the sea appears half-way up the mountain slopes; but on, south of Iceland so that you may have birds and whales from it.

It is simple in the telling, but one should not forget that the first Vikings to undertake such voyages were sailing into the unknown.

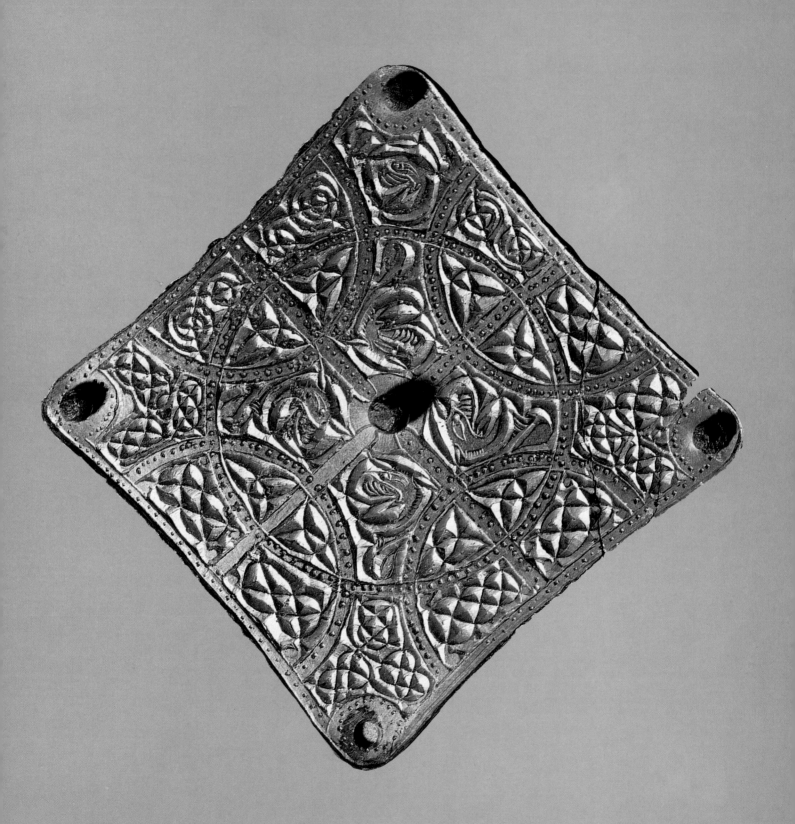

3 Traders and Looters

In 841 Rouen was attacked by Danish raiders who are said to have carried everywhere 'a fury of rapine, fire and sword, they gave up the city, the monks and the rest of the people to carnage and captivity. Some of the monasteries and other places near the Seine they devastated, the rest they filled with terror, having received much money'. Such entries in Frankish and other west European chronicles contain their exaggerations, but a number of points emerge so clearly that there can be no reason to doubt them. The Viking fury was unleashed not only against monasteries, but also cities and villages. As a result, monks and others were carried off into captivity, but Viking devastations were sometimes prevented by the payment of 'much money', to make them depart with their captives and their plunder.

Captives might be ransomed, if they were of sufficient importance to the monastery or community from which they had been seized, and so converted into cash. The others were destined for a life of hard labour in the Scandinavians' homelands or their settlements overseas, if not consigned for sale in the slave-market for silver or other goods.

Tribute was extorted in vast sums during the ninth century from the Franks (as it was to be at a later date from the Anglo-Saxons). For instance, in 845 Charles 'the Bald' is recorded as having paid £7,000 in silver to rid the Seine Valley of Viking raiders. The total references in the Frankish sources to such payments amount to 685 lb of gold and 43,042 lb of silver, and if some sums are exaggerated, there are no doubt others that have gone unrecorded. At the same time similar raids for loot, and occasionally for tribute, were taking place in England. The numbers of the Vikings involved in these attacks may not have been large, but there is no doubt of the damage that they inflicted and the wealth that they secured for themselves.

Remarkably little of this treasure has been found in Scandinavia in the form of the coins in which the tribute must have been paid. The ninth-century Hon hoard from Norway (92) contains Carolingian coins mounted for use on a necklace, and among the other objects that go to make up its weight of 5½ lb of gold is a large trefoil-shaped mount of Carolingian work and an Anglo-Saxon finger-ring. Much of the gold and silver will have been melted down to make ornaments, which would still have served as a man's capital, but many Vikings may have used their new wealth to purchase land, or to equip themselves with ships and other necessities to become merchants, or to set out as settlers to the new lands in the west.

Carolingian and Anglo-Saxon coins are thus found in the areas of Scandinavian settlement in Celtic Britain and Ireland. The massive

10 *Anglo-Saxon book-mount looted by a Norwegian Viking.*

Cuerdale treasure-chest, hidden in about 903, contained some thousand Frankish coins among its total of over seven thousand. This 88 lb hoard (over four times larger than any other Viking hoard from Britain or Scandinavia) may well have been brought together by Vikings who had recently fled Ireland for north-west England, where they concealed it in a bank of the River Ribble in fear of some threat. One can only speculate as to what it could have been, and what its outcome, for them to have left such a fantastic treasure unreclaimed – it was discovered only in 1840 by workmen engaged on repairs to the river-bank (1).

The largest known hoard of Viking gold weighed over 10 lb when it was buried in Ireland, on a small island up the River Shannon, sometime in the late ninth or early tenth century, to judge by the surviving descriptions of the objects, all arm-rings, which sadly were melted down in the early nineteenth century.

The Viking raiders who settled in Scotland and Ireland would have brought this wealth of gold and silver with them. For these were lands without coinage of their own, and without regular supplies of precious metal. The gold and silver that they did have was used in small quantities and the latter was often of poor quality, having been debased by the addition of other metals.

The finest British and Irish objects did, of course, fall into Viking hands by one means or another. But most of such eighth- and ninth-century objects found in Viking-Age graves in Scandinavia, and on sites such as Kaupang and Helgö (108), are of bronze. Some of them are highly ornamented, many of them would have been gilt: they should probably be seen as curiosities – souvenirs even – of the Viking expeditions west-over-sea, removed from caskets, shrines and holy book-covers (10). Some mounts had pins attached to them to convert them into brooches for the wives and sweethearts left behind to run the farm, during the summer's raiding and trading. One such example, found at Romfø in Norway, of gilt-bronze with amber and blue glass settings, is splendidly decorated with bosses, monsters and animal ornament (11).

Other objects were carried carefully home to Scandinavia so that they might be used for the purpose for which they had been made. Such were the fine wooden bucket with enamel mounts in the Oseberg ship-burial, or that clad in ornamented bronze sheets found in a woman's grave at Birka.

A little house-shaped casket from Norway (preserved in Copenhagen) was made in the eighth or early ninth century in Scotland in order to hold saints' relics (12). How and why did such a shrine cross the North Sea? It has never been buried and still contains relics, although these are now of post-Viking date. Was it brought over by an early convert as a gift to a Norwegian church (presumably in the eleventh century)? If so, one is left wondering why there should be runes carved on its base stating: RANVAIK A KISTU THASA (Ranvaig owns this casket). Was it, after all, looted by a pagan Viking as a jewel-box for his lady? It would then be a curious coincidence for it to have reverted to its original use.

The ninth century saw the Vikings in the west raiding even further afield than the shores of Britain and France. Two expeditions are known to

11 ABOVE RIGHT *Monsters ornament a Celtic mount adapted for use as a Viking brooch.*

12 BELOW RIGHT *A house-shaped casket for Christian relics carried off to Norway from the British Isles.*

have plundered in the Iberian Peninsula. The second lasted from 859 to 862 and much of that time was spent in the western Mediterranean, with ships raiding North Africa, the South of France, and Italy.

The main flow of silver into Scandinavia between the late ninth and the late tenth century came not from the west, but from the east, in the form of Arabic coins. The trading-links between Scandinavia and the Islamic territory to the south and east of the Caucasus and the Caspian Sea are described below. Well over sixty-thousand such coins have been found in Scandinavia, and others were passed on to reach the British Isles; some have even been found in Iceland. But many more must have been melted down to make neck-rings, brooches and all manner of other ornaments. The circulation of so much treasure in and around the Baltic at that time meant that home-based Vikings who wished to engage in piracy might make fat pickings without having to stir very far afield in the process.

This supply of Arabic silver dwindled to a trickle during the latter part of the tenth century, when the trade-routes may have been interrupted. But their silver-mines were anyway nearly exhausted and the supply to Scandinavia dried up altogether at the beginning of the eleventh century. The Vikings were forced to look elsewhere for sources of silver to supply the quantities to which they had become accustomed. Fortunately for Europe there were German silver-mines in the Harz Mountains that were increasingly exploited from the mid tenth century. Some seventy thousand coins from German mints have been found in Scandinavia, dating to the late tenth and eleventh centuries, together with well over forty thousand from England. Viking raids on England began again in earnest at the end of the tenth century, leading ultimately to conquest. Massive tribute was extorted over a thirty-year period amounting to tens of millions of coins of which these finds are but the remainder.

With over a thousand hoards known from Scandinavia, we should ask just what *did* silver mean to the Vikings, who went to such lengths to acquire it in these quantities. Its one obvious function was for display, as an outward sign of the success of its wearer. It was considered as family wealth, like land, and no more than a small object or two would be buried with the dead. It was used to reward retainers and to provide lavish hospitality, for generosity in such matters was a quality greatly admired by the Vikings and assured a man's esteem among his fellows. If spent on land, it might enable a man to rise above his station as a freeman; for a slave, it could mean his liberty.

National coinages did not become firmly established in Scandinavia until the eleventh century. During the ninth and tenth centuries coins were for the most part regarded merely as lumps of silver – occasionally pretty enough to be worth mounting on necklaces (55) – that had to be tested for purity by scratching or nicking their surfaces, and weighed in a balance before use in commercial transactions.

Portable balances were carried by all serious merchants. These were ingeniously designed to fold up, so as to occupy the minimum amount of space when not in use. Their arms fold inwards and fit within one of the pans, which in turn nests in the other; the whole is then protected by a hemispherical bronze box that would have been carried in a pouch. A regulated set of weights was required; these might be simple lumps of lead, like those found together with the scales from Jåtten in Norway, complete with their own linen bag. On the other hand weights might be ornamented in various ways, as is the case with an unusually fine set from a man's grave at Kiloran Bay, on the island of Colonsay off the west coast of Scotland (13). These will have been made somewhere in the British Isles, for several of the lead pieces are capped with scraps of Celtic or Anglo-Saxon metalwork, cut from other objects. This is even the case with the two remarkable enamel mounts that are decorated with motifs thought to imitate letters of the Cufic script, as found on the imported Arabic coins.

13 *Ornamented weights for Viking balance-scales.*

In such an economy, which required silver to be weighed before use in commerce, it was not necessary to keep all one's silver resources in the form of coin. If, in mid-transaction, one suddenly found oneself short of a small amount of silver to complete a deal, all that was necessary was to cut the end off one's arm-ring or brooch to make up the desired weight. Here then is the explanation for the fact that so many Viking silver hoards, from Cuerdale (1) to Birka (18) and beyond, consist of a mixture of complete ornaments and coins together with so-called 'hack-silver' – their cut-up fragments. Hack-silver would have been in continuous demand all the time that silver was valued by the Vikings for commercial purposes and coins were not used as counted money. But silver, in whatever form, had to be buried for safe-keeping in an age when there were no strong-rooms. So today when hoards are found by chance, it is only because their original owners died without having passed on their secret.

Carolingian and Anglo-Saxon merchants would have been reluctant to accept handfuls of hack-silver in return for their commodities because both dealt in controlled currencies. Scandinavian merchants based in Ireland in the tenth century, primarily on Dublin, were clearly hoarding Anglo-Saxon coins (mostly minted in Chester) for use when they went trading in England. In the same way, one might expect that some of the ninth-century Frankish tribute found its way back to the country of its origin in payment for the many imported goods from the Carolingian Empire that are found in Scandinavia.

Trading connections between the Frankish world and Scandinavia stretch back long before this period and would not necessarily have been much interrupted by the activities of the raiders. Of early Viking-Age date is the Fejø cup (14) found in Denmark, but such a piece of Carolingian metalwork might as well have been looted as traded. Wine was imported from the Rhineland into Scandinavia in some quantity for those who could afford it, no doubt by way of Hedeby where actual casks have been found reused as the linings for wells. Other luxuries that may have been associated with this wine-trade are pottery jugs and drinking-glasses, like several found in graves at Birka (15a). Superior sword-blades made by

14 LEFT *A Carolingian cup found in Denmark.*

15a RIGHT *A wine jug and glass beaker from the Rhineland, exported to Birka.*

Rhenish smiths were also in demand throughout Scandinavia (although there were attempts made by the Carolingian authorities to control this trade because of the unfortunate repercussions it could have on the Franks themselves!). Frankish ornaments (15b) were among other imports and had some influence on the products of Scandinavian jewellers. Desirable goods of a more mundane nature, which are known to have passed through Hedeby, included quernstones made of lava from the Eifel region of Germany.

Some Vikings may have devoted themselves to commerce, but the rôle of merchant was one among several for many of those who owned a ship and who could thus venture abroad. Such a man was Ottar the Norwegian, more often known as Ohthere from the Anglo-Saxon version of his name. He visited England and the court of King Alfred sometime in the 870s, when an account of his activities was recorded. He lived in the far north of Norway where he farmed a little, tamed reindeer, hunted whales and walrus, and exacted tribute from the Lapps, who lived still further north. With the proceeds of these various occupations he went trading (most especially with the Lappish tribute, which took the form of furs, skins, down, walrus ivory, and ropes made of hide). Ottar sailed southwards down the Norwegian coast, taking a month to reach a trading-place now identified with Kaupang, on the west side of the Oslo Fjord.

Kaupang flourished in the ninth century as a local market-place, but one that had international connections. Imports of Rhenish pottery and glass have been found there, as have bronzes and enamelled mounts from the British Isles. Its exports probably included Norwegian soapstone bowls and schist for whetstones, the remains of which have been found in quantity on the settlement. Iron-smelting, bronze-working and bead-making were among the other activities carried out at Kaupang, although not necessarily all the year round. Its many wealthy graves, and those of its hinterland, appear to be of merchant-farmers. Kaupang (the name meant 'market-place') is thus likely to have been a seasonal trading-centre, one that for some reason never grew and prospered to the extent of Hedeby and Birka. Indeed, Norway lacked such towns in the tenth century; Oslo, Bergen and Trondheim are all late Viking-Age foundations.

Continuing his journey southwards, Ottar eventually arrived, five days after setting out from Kaupang, at Hedeby. This southern Danish port lay on an inlet of the River Schlei and thus had direct access to the Baltic. It was this commanding position, at the base of the narrow Jutland Peninsula, that accounted for its development as the focus for the transit trade between the countries of western Europe and the Baltic during the ninth and tenth centuries. It was established at the beginning of the ninth century, protected by a small fort, which overlooks the site, and by ramparts which were built during the tenth century. Hedeby grew to become the largest of the Scandinavian Viking-Age towns. It was far more than just an import/export centre; throughout the sixty-acre site enclosed by the rampart evidence has been found for many industries and crafts, from weaving and potting to iron-smelting and fine metalworking, from the working of leather to the manufacture of glass beads.

15b LEFT *Frankish belt-mounts ornamented with foliage patterns, found in Sweden.*

Fig. 3 OVERLEAF *A map of the Viking world.*

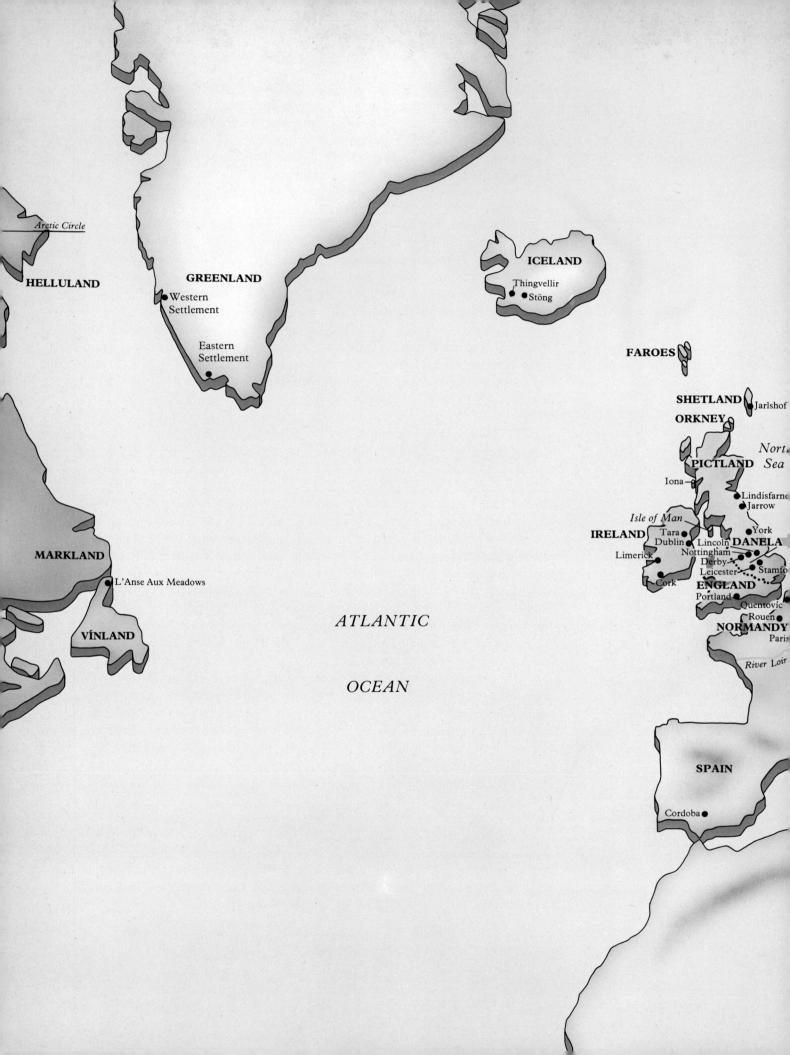

ARCTIC OCEAN

Arctic Circle

White Sea

NORWAY

SWEDEN

Lake Ladoga

Gulf of Finland

Staraja Ladoga

Kaupang

Birka

Baltic
Sea

River Volkhov

Novgorod

Jaroslavl

Bolgar

DENMARK

Grobin

River Dvina

River Oka

Ribe

edeby

Wiskiauten

Smolensk

Hamburg

Wolin

Truso

Gnezdovo

Bremen

River Vistula

orestad

River Elbe

Chernigov

River Rhine

Mainz

Prague

Cracow

Kiev

River Volga

River Dniepr

River Don

Berezanji

Itil

River Danube

Aral
Sea

Rome

Black Sea

Caspian
Sea

Byzantium

Tashkent

Piraeus
(Athens)

Samarkand

River Tigris

Gurgan

Mediterranean Sea

River Euphrates

Damascus

Baghdad

Jerusalem

Persian Gulf

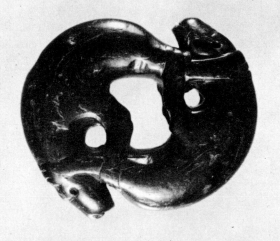

The Norwegians were also prominent in the North Sea and Atlantic, and their most important trading settlement in this area must have been Dublin, a Scandinavian foundation that was exceptionally active and successful in the tenth and eleventh centuries, as recent excavations have shown. Dublin was the focal point on the western trade-routes that linked the Atlantic islands with Scandinavia and western Europe. Its wealth supported craftsmen and artists of many kinds (86). From about 997 it had its own mint, the first in Ireland. Other important towns founded by the Scandinavians in Ireland were Cork and Limerick, but no traces of these have yet been found below the modern cities.

The Vikings met with no towns in Scotland, neither did they establish any. In England, on the other hand, they were able to take over existing Anglo-Saxon towns, like Lincoln and York. The latter was the seat of a series of Norwegian and Danish kings for nearly eighty years during the ninth and tenth centuries. New excavations have produced extensive evidence for craftsmen and their workshops (31); wood, metal, leather, stone, jet and amber were all materials being worked in this thriving Anglo-Scandinavian community. Old and new finds of Scandinavian objects (77) serve to demonstrate its cosmopolitan character and its contacts across the North Sea; one possible export, among many, was jet derived from the near-by source at Whitby (16).

The earliest trading- and manufacturing-centres in Sweden, Denmark and the Baltic were at small settlements such as Paviken on Gotland, and Ribe on the west coast of Jutland. Recent excavations have taken place at both these sites. Ship-repairing and bead-making were among the activities carried out at Paviken at the beginning of the Viking period, while workshops of similar date have been found at Ribe, both for bead-making and for casting bronze brooches. But the earliest such centre known was at Helgö, a settlement founded on an island in Lake Mälar in the third century AD which continued in existence up to and well within the Viking Age. Excavations at Helgö have produced a remarkable quantity of metalworkers' debris and evidence of widespread foreign contacts (e.g. 108). It seems that Helgö was one of the predecessors of Birka, whose development involved a shift to a larger site a few miles away, in order to exploit the opening-up of the trade-routes to the riches of the east.

Like Hedeby, Birka commenced its life as an important trading-centre at the beginning of the ninth century, situated on an island in the great Mälar Lake of east-central Sweden. Although the smaller of the two (its population has been guessed at seven hundred to a thousand inhabitants), Birka also was protected by a small fort and was eventually enclosed by a semicircular rampart. There was a choice of three harbours for merchants' ships, but Birka was probably also important for winter traders (particularly of furs), as it could easily have been approached over the ice, on skates or sledges. Only a small part of the settlement-area at Birka has been excavated, but it has produced evidence for the usual urban crafts, particularly bone- and metalworking (79).

Birka was the major destination of goods brought from the east, but it also had trading relations with the west. The regular appearance in

16 *Animals carved from imported jet, found in Norway.*

17 OVERLEAF *Birka: fort and rampart of Sweden's foremost Viking town.*

eastern Sweden of Cufic silver coins from the Islamic east, commenced in the 790s and defines the beginning of the Viking Age in the Baltic. Many of the several thousand graves at Birka have been excavated to reveal a collection of rich and remarkable objects, including many from the east: glass, silk, trinkets, coins, and from the settlement deposits, fragmentary remains of much more. In the late tenth century Birka's fortunes declined (as did those of Hedeby), but an important silver hoard (18), buried about 975, is among the latest finds from the site.

From the last quarter of the tenth century trade-routes with the east were interrupted and they never recovered. Birka slowly collapsed during the 970s, and its place as commercial centre of Uppland was taken over by Sigtuna to the north. Gotland came to dominate the Baltic trade. The Swedes had over many centuries developed contacts with the east. The runestones in the province of Uppland, in which Birka is situated, commemorate expeditions to the east. A group of early eleventh-century memorials record those who never returned from an expedition to Serkland (the Caliphate of Baghdad), led by Ingvar 'the far-travelled'. One of the band had interestingly 'been long in the west'.

The island of Gotland, lying centrally in the Baltic, was prominent in trade with the east, and with the west Baltic, and supported a rich and independent farming community. Shelving beaches made many natural harbours suitable for traffic with shallow-draught vessels, allowing naturally good communications to develop in all directions. Gotland was an entrepôt deriving its wealth from the handling and transit trade. All over the island rich graves and buried treasures suggest independent participation by Gotlandic farmers in this rich trade. Large amounts of imported silver have been found as hoards of coins, hacked-up silver objects or jewellery buried by men who never claimed them again. Whether they died on the island or abroad is unknown, but the 40,000 Arabic, 38,000 German and 21,000 Anglo-Saxon silver coins which have been found there, are evidence of the activity of the inhabitants.

On Gotland and beyond have been found objects from other east Baltic groups. Pieces of their jewellery are sometimes easily recognisable from their characteristic form or decoration. A late Viking-Age silver chain with large geometric pendants from Eidet in northern Norway is Finnish, demonstrating trade contacts across the far north. The bronze horseheads on a fire-steel from Åse in Norway are very typical of a Finnish zoomorphic style of decoration. Scattered in the west Baltic area are a few pieces of jewellery from among the Balts living between the Finns and the western Slavs, on the south-east Baltic coast.

In the territory of the western Slavs (including present-day Poland and the German Democratic Republic) the Vikings traded in native urban communities along the southern Baltic coast, where craft activities were similar to those in Scandinavian towns. Economic development had already taken place in these western Slav areas, and this provided a very useful basis for the Viking traders to exploit. Settlements and burials along the coast and further inland suggest that Scandinavian mercenaries and

18 *Silver ornaments, coins and hack-silver buried together, about 975, in the Swedish town of Birka.*

traders formed small groups in the larger communities, and that their rôle was complex and changed over time.

Pottery among the Scandinavians was not highly developed, either technically or aesthetically and high-quality material was occasionally brought from Slav areas, such as a stamped pot found at the Danish ring fort of Trelleborg which probably came from present-day Mecklenburg. The south Baltic may have been a rich source of grain, as suggested by late Viking-Age finds from Denmark, for it has been supposed that barriers imposed by the emerging political units created unequal values even on basic food commodities. It has also been suggested that peasant taxes might have been tendered in high-quality grain which could then be traded.

Dynastic marriages took place between western Slavs and Danes in the late Viking period, and Slavs mounted piratical raids on Danish settlements. Imports into Scandinavia from these areas included silver jewellery of a totally different style from the native material. Earrings with light openwork and delicate filigree decoration or with embossed globular shapes are characteristic. Lunate silver pendants and hollow beads with the most delicate of filigree and granulation work are outstanding (19). The Slav earrings may have been looted or brought back as souvenirs, then worn by a Viking's sweetheart; but the use of silver toe-rings by women is a likely eastern custom, and the pair from the Danish site of Fyrkat represents a fashion unlikely to have been adopted by Scandinavians.

At Birka an eastern warrior was buried, sitting in his chamber grave, along with a hammer-axe, armour-piercing arrows and a fur hat with silver tassels. His other possessions included a glass vessel, and scales. We may imagine that other exotic foreigners lived and travelled in Scandinavia. Anglo-Saxon moneyers are identified from their names on coins struck at Lund. Arab and Jewish merchants and traders visited the emporia of northern Europe and several of their written accounts survive. Ibrahim al-Tartushi visited a town that was probably Hedeby about AD 950: 'the town is poorly provided with property or treasure. The inhabitants' principal food is fish which is very plentiful. The people often throw a newborn child into the sea rather than maintain it. Furthermore women have the right to claim a divorce; they do this themselves whenever they wish. There is also an artificial makeup for the eyes: when they use it beauty never fades; on the contrary it increases in men and women as well'.

From the later seventh century and continuing into the eighth, groups from Gotland and Uppland began to settle on the east Baltic coast. Transport over the massive distances involved in reaching eastern trading-centres was along the river systems. Scandinavian settlements were strategically placed to control the lower courses of these rivers flowing through Estonia and Latvia into the Baltic. Later routes southwards across Poland and western Russia, deep penetrating rivers such as the Dvina or Weichsel could lead to the Upper Dniepr, Kiev and the Black Sea. Later, land routes began to be used so intensively that these routes and the settlements built on them started to decline. The main route led from the Gulf of Finland via the River Neva to Lake Ladoga

19 *The delicacy of silver jewellery: ear-rings and a pendant from western Slav lands, and a crystal necklace, found in Sweden.*

where there developed a major trading settlement, Staraja Ladoga, known to the Scandinavians as Aldeigjuborg.

From Lake Ladoga there opened up two major water-routes. One led eastwards through Jaroslavl on the upper waters of the River Volga, and so south-east to Bolgar. From here the river led on to the Sea of Azov or to the trading-centre of Itil on the Caspian Sea. A second, directly southern, route lay via the rivers Volkhov and Lovat to the Upper Dniepr and so via Kiev to the Black Sea coast. Further down this route at Smolensk or Chernigov it was possible to head east to the Upper Oka River and so pick up the Volga route to Bolgar. A Scandinavian oval brooch from the Moscow area is evidence for contact by this route. Kiev was an important centre which developed a powerful culture based on commercial contacts with Byzantium. Communication overland from central Europe linked Kiev to Cracow and Mainz so that contact was maintained independently of the Baltic route, while an eastern route led to the Caspian Sea.

At one point on the River Dniepr between Kiev and the Black Sea, a land portage over the steppe was necessary. The Byzantine Emperor Constantine Porphyrogenitos in the mid tenth century records the difficulties of this fifth cataract: 'All the ships stop with the stems pointing towards the shore, and those with a crew who had been chosen to watch go ashore and . . . they keep a sharp lookout because of the Pechenegs; but the others put the goods ashore, and also the slaves who are chained, and walk six miles until they have passed the cataract. Then they take their boats past the falls partly by towing them, partly by carrying them on their shoulders. There they embark and continue their voyage.' At the end of the river journey, at Berezanji, the Black Sea was within easy reach, and proof that Scandinavians did penetrate this far is provided by a runic inscription from the area.

Recent research shows that much economic and social development had taken place among the eastern Slavs before the Scandinavians arrived. It seems likely that the Vikings stimulated and expanded trade here, as they did in western Slav areas, extending the trade-routes to the Gulf of Finland, and hence to Scandinavia. They supplied an existing demand by ruthlessly exploiting the slave-trade, and systematically intensifying the hunting of furs to satisfy an eastern luxury market. A group of spiral silver armlets with polyhedral terminals, so-called 'Permian rings', after a forest area in north Russia which produced many furs, may be remains of activity in this sphere (20). Scandinavians were not alone in their activities, for the Finns, an Ugrian-speaking people who occupied parts of the north Russian forest zone, seemed to have actively engaged in trading themselves. Their remains are found in the lowest level in the town of Staraja Ladoga. In many sources the name 'Rus' is applied by Arabs and Byzantines to foreigners trading from the north, and more particularly to groups based at Kiev. While they are distinguished from Slavs, their exact antecedents remain a problem. As in so many areas, the Scandinavians probably adopted many native customs and became part of a vigorous mixed group involved in aggressive trading.

Places like Bolgar on the Middle Volga developed as bazaars, terminals

20 *Silver neck-rings, and spiral rings from Russia, buried together on Öland.*

for caravan-routes leading to central Asia and China. Here the Scandinavians brought furs, slaves, wax and Frankish swords. We do not know if the Scandinavians travelled further to more exotic lands, but they must have learned of them from merchants. Further south the Vikings made direct contact with the Muslim Arab, Jewish Khazar and Christian Byzantine cultures. These advanced and sophisticated societies provided, directly or indirectly, luxuries superior to those that the west could offer: embroidered silks, glass vessels, delicately glazed pottery, silver and bronze vessels decorated with exotic inscriptions or art motifs (21). A hoard of silver coins from Fittja in Uppland contains silver minted at Cordoba in the west, in Egypt, Damascus, Isfahan, Baghdad and Tashkent in the east; the contacts established by the Vikings via the Muslim world were very wide-ranging indeed.

The danger of the journeys and the desirability of the goods made the profits on long-distance trade enormous. So important was this trade that on several occasions Kievan forces attacked Byzantium to gain trade concessions. Of some prized items little now survives. Fragments of gold-embroidered silk from Lund (22) and Mammen may have come originally from Byzantium, as also the silver edgings from Valsgärde. At Birka over forty male graves held silk clothing, some of it embroidered. An oriental jacket with embroidered facings and tassels was found at Birka in a man's grave, and at Vårby gilt-silver eastern mounts originally for a belt, along with eastern as well as Scandinavian style pendants (23). The necklace from Hämeenlinna with its oriental silver pendants and reused Cufic coins has the feel of accumulated souvenirs.

Perhaps the Middle Eastern bronze incense-burner from Åbyn was

21 LEFT *Exotic eastern vessels found in Sweden: a bronze flask, silver bowl, and glazed cup.*

22 BELOW *Gold-embroidered silk, perhaps from Byzantium, found in Lund.*

23 OVERLEAF *The Vårby belt-mounts and pendants.*

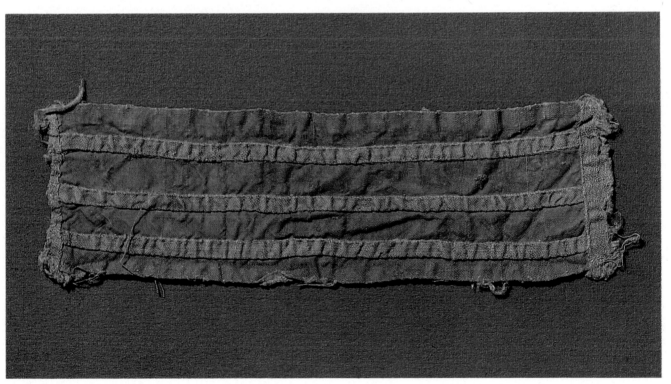

used for its original purpose in some Swedish longhouse. An interesting group of Byzantine objects from Hedeby raises several problems. The Byzantine lead seal is a difficult piece to explain. Was it brought as a souvenir, or attached to a bale? And did it come from across the Baltic and along Russian river-routes, or via Italy? With the silver reliquary capsule on its chain from Allmänninge and the Norsborg pendant cross, both of Kievan workmanship, it is an open question whether the Scandinavian wearers had been converted to the Christian faith this jewellery proclaimed, or were insensible to it. The brightly glazed pottery egg from Sigtuna is another piece of Kievan origin, related to the Orthodox celebration of Easter. Several others are known from Lund, but whether they served their primary purpose is unknown. Above all it was silver coins that the merchants took back to Scandinavia from the Muslim Arab world.

During the later part of the period Viking trade with the east declined and the shift of European trade-routes deprived the Baltic route of much of its earlier significance. The Scandinavians still maintained an active interest in the east however; at the court of Byzantium Vikings had for a long time served as mercenaries in the military. In about AD 1000 they were formally organised into an imperial guard. Membership of the Varangian Guard, as it was called, would still earn a Viking much prestige at home.

With their conversion to Christianity, the Vikings forged new links and when we read of Scandinavians making the pilgrimage to Jerusalem, it is clear that the Vikings had accepted a new life and had found ways of co-existing peacefully with their fellow Christians from all over western Europe.

24 *Christian objects of Kievan origin, found in Sweden.*

4 Viking Settlement

In the Viking Age, as before and long after, the vast majority of people in northern Europe lived by tilling the land and grazing livestock. Urban settlement depended on the production of a food surplus in the countryside. Hunting and fishing were valuable resources and formed a very important supplement to the diet; honey, eggs or wild plants were gathered where possible. The relative importance of each activity depended on the total resources of each locality.

A range of artefacts connected with fishing survives. Stone sinkers and bark floats were used with nets, and some fragments of them do survive. Fish-traps are known, while hooks and small sinkers show that line-fishing was practised; a finely incised whalebone line-winder from north Norway implies some long lines (25). Spears and forks, often complex pieces of iron-smithing, represent another method of fishing. At sea, seals and walrus were hunted, and whales driven ashore. A variety of iron hunting gear reflects the different quarry which was speared or shot with arrows. Since furs and skins were widely sought, it was essential to do as little damage as possible. But little organic material, such as traps and containers, survives as evidence of these activities.

The tools of the farmer are the main evidence remaining for farming methods (26), but carbonised grain and animal bones have also been preserved. After about AD 600 we can identify few typological changes until the medieval period, and the precise date of many artefacts is sometimes not known. However, while points of detail are uncertain the outlines are clear.

A written source, possibly from the Viking Age, the *Rígsthula*, refers to the farmer's life: 'He tamed the oxen, tempered ploughshares, timbered houses and barns for the hay, fashioned carts, and followed the plough'. The forest had to be cleared by the axe, and brushwood burnt off; roots were then dug out and stones cleared. Next, the field had to be ploughed. The simplest plough was the ard, which had two handles to guide its central beam and a symmetrical iron blade to cut the furrow. On light soils this primitive instrument was adequate, but for heavy soils a stronger plough was required with a coulter to cut, heavy share to lift, and mouldboard to turn the sod. A plough like this may have been used from the late Viking period, as at Lindholm Høje, where a field was blown over by sand and partly preserved. Horses or oxen could be used for plough traction on larger fields, but where land was scarce and small plots were cultivated, the spade and hoe were important tools.

Crops such as rye, oats, wheat and barley were grown, their relative importance depending on local conditions. Grain was harvested by cutting

25 *A whalebone line-winder incised with the figure of a bird.*

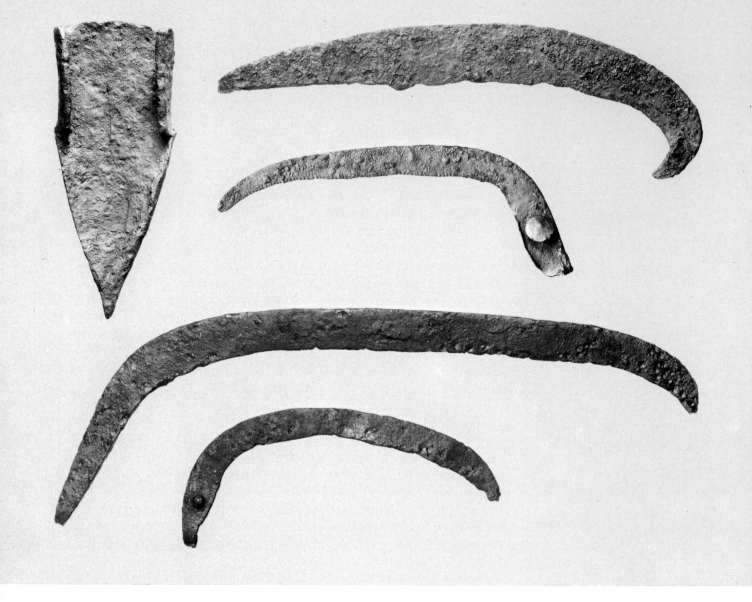

the ear from the stalk with a curved sickle, while a similar tool with a straighter, serrated edge suggests that a sawing motion was sometimes employed. After separating the grain from the chaff and drying it for storage, it would be ground to flour by hand on rotary quernstones. Grit from the heavy stones often tended to crumble into the flour, and ground-down teeth were a result, as shown by examination of skeletal remains.

Grasses and hay would have been cut with a long scythe for use as winter fodder and bedding for animals. Another source of animal foodstuff and bedding was foliage and shoots from trees and shrubs, cut down with a hook-ended leaf-knife. Keeping farm animals alive over the winter was of crucial importance. Weak animals, and others for whom there would be no winter fodder, were slaughtered to ensure adequate supplies for the rest. Meat not eaten at the subsequent feasting would be preserved for the winter by salting, drying or smoking.

26 Iron tools of the Viking-Age farmer in Norway.

As pressure on resources grew, the practice of transhumance (driving herds to summer-pastures in uplands, and wintering them in lowland areas) developed in Norway. The use of shielings for sheep also developed. The generally small size of animals in the Viking Age reflects a low level of nourishment and the lack of widespread selective breeding. Pigs, geese and fowl were also kept. One of the triumphs of colonisation of the new lands to the west was the successful transport aboard ship of the horses, cattle, sheep and smaller domesticated animals that made up the farmyard community. Grazing grain-stubble was one supplementary source of cattle feed while the cattle in turn provided dung to fertilise the fields. Forks and shovels suggest that dung was systematically spread to increase crop yields, and crops might also be rotated to prevent impoverishment of the soil.

Large numbers of freemen lived each on his own farm, working it with his family, which often extended to several generations. Slaves or unfree men might undertake the heavier labour, and free labourers might work for their keep and a small reward, herding or minding the flocks and in less specialised work. A rich man who owned a large estate would probably employ numerous men and women in subsistence activities, such as cloth-weaving. This would leave him leisure for part of the year to join raiding parties or trade on his own account. The amount of land owned, and a man's status, could change in a series of bad years when the smaller, less prosperous farmer might have to borrow from his more fortunate neighbour. Obligation in many forms would often bind a lesser man to the protection of a greater, whom he in turn would have to support. And in litigation over land inheritance or to exact redress, when force or the threat of it was needed to execute a judgement, such mutual bonds were important.

The character of rural settlements and their distribution varied greatly, depending on conditions. Temporary settlements were sometimes established to work seasonally in high mountain pastures, for fishing in rivers, or digging bog-iron. Caves might have been used for shelter, or small clusters of rude huts. Main settlement areas were on the richer agricultural land; the more productive it was the denser the settlement. Usually each farming unit lay isolated, a cluster of dwellings, huts and outhouses. Specialised activities such as iron-smithing or storage would often take place in outbuildings. Although varying with the limitation of building material, this general arrangement was widespread. Some farms had only one building, but the more wealthy a community the more complex was its organisation. In the late Viking Age groups of farms occur in village-like communities, especially in Denmark.

In the eleventh-century settlement at Lindholm Høje there was some metalworking, and at Eketorp on the Swedish island of Öland manufacturing and trading took place in the circular, defended settlement. Trading and craft-working centres, which had rarely appeared in Scandinavia before the Viking Age, increased in number during the period (pp. 131–50). Their influence on the rural areas grew as their numbers increased and their trading activity became more complex.

The farming community generally tried to be self-sufficient in basic necessities, but specialised services, raw materials, trinkets and luxuries might be brought in. This was increasingly so in the later Viking Age. Natural barriers such as forests, bogs or mountains might intervene to isolate settlements from each other. A feast, wedding or the arrival of pedlars would break the isolation, which in winter could be extreme. But in the Viking period there is evidence for advances in transport by land as well as sea. Towards the end of the period communications were improved by marking and paving fords, marking the lines of trackways, and building bridges. The needs of a more developed political organisation accounted for this, as well as the growing volume of trade and necessity for regular attendance at church in all seasons.

27 *Transport over the winter ice: bone skates and iron spikes, from Lund.*

In the winter, waterways turned to ice and for traversing them a range of bone skates and iron shoe-spikes are known (27). Spikes for the feet of horses show that they, too, went over the ice. Skis were used to travel across the snow, while a range of sledges could be used to transport loads across snow, ice and grass. Wagons with sturdy wheels and a body that could be unfastened from a frame transported bulk loads, and perhaps important people. The most elaborately carved sledges and a wagon were contained in the female burial at Oseberg. Some vehicles might be pulled by oxen or horses, and a series of elaborate horse-collars (28) and jangling iron fastenings are associated with this form of transport. Riding-gear such as elaborate iron bridles, richly inlaid spurs and stirrups (66), and bridle mounts of exceptional artistry (87) were a medium for the expression of social prestige. Iron horseshoes begin to appear in the late Viking Age.

It was with this background that in the late eighth, the ninth and the tenth centuries Scandinavian peoples flooded eastward and westward from their homelands. Part of their motive was to find new lands to settle, where they could earn their living. They founded new settlements or became established in existing communities from the coast of Newfoundland in the west to Yaroslavl in northern Russia, and from Arctic Norway to the coasts of northern France.

These scattered colonies varied greatly in size and character. In some areas such as England there was already a relatively dense population, and a variety of Scandinavian groups imposed themselves as lords, craftsmen, or peasant farmers. Iceland, by contrast, was effectively empty when the Vikings began to arrive, and their settlement was purely agricultural. Varying motives drove different social groups from their Scandinavian homeland, and they had different expectations of the territories they settled. Sometimes individuals filled specialised occupations – trading or serving as mercenary soldiers. Their rate of absorption into local communities was influenced by whether they travelled in families or sought out local women to marry.

One aspect of Viking settlement, the far-flung voyages westward across uncharted oceans to inhospitable new lands, has great romantic appeal, but we sometimes hear of those who never reached their intended destination: in the first colonisation of Greenland only fourteen out of twenty-five ships arrived from Iceland. The motives which drove families to settle permanently away from their native land, however, were not romantic. Population pressure resulted in a scarcity of cultivable land in some areas, and increasing use of marginal land led to the ever-present spectre of famine in a bad year. The forcible imposition of more control by Scandinavian chiefs alienated some families, who could only resist and, if defeated, leave. Individual fugitives from feuds or from justice had often to sneak away.

Geography and the search for a suitable, familiar environment played a part in determining the direction of early Viking expansion overseas. At the end of the eighth century Norwegian farming groups colonised the islands of Shetland and Orkney lying along a direct sea-route from western Norway to Scotland. The Faeroes far to the north-west began to be settled at this time. Similar in landscape to western Norway, the islands could support a high level of sheep-farming. Fishing, fowling and hunting whales supplemented this, while products such as sealskin could be traded. The south Shetland settlement at Jarlshof, consisting of its turf and stone longhouses, was sited by a beach on a sheltered bay. The majority of the communities appear to have been subsistence farmers who had few luxuries. The logical progression was southwards to the north-west coast of Scotland and the Hebrides, which, seen from a Norwegian perspective, are 'the Southern Islands'. It was from these settlements that some Norwegians raided the coastal churches and monasteries of northern Britain. Entry into the Irish Sea area – the eastern coasts of Ireland, north-west England and Wales – was the next step.

Norwegian attacks on Ireland began in the late eighth century, and soon fortified bases were established on the coasts and river estuaries, enabling raids to be widely mounted. In the mid ninth century a base at Dublin was established which grew into an important settlement, as is shown by rich finds from the near-by cemetery at Islandbridge – Kilmainham. From the

850s the Scandinavian bands included both Norwegians and Danes. Sometimes they co-operated; sometimes they fought each other for spoils, or became involved in Irish internecine feuding.

The Vikings also established other coastal bases, such as Cork and Limerick, while Dublin became the centre of a kingdom based on a rich and extensive trade. As in other Viking towns there were varied craft and manufacturing activities. There were no native towns and, despite growing Irish political domination, they remained largely Scandinavian in character. There was little Scandinavian rural settlement, in contrast to England, and widespread finds of Viking silver are due to considerable inland trade. The largest known Viking gold hoard (about 10 lb in weight) comes from an island in the River Shannon. There were several episodes of political reverses when, with their Irish slaves and concubines, Scandinavians left for other areas, notably Iceland. In 980 defeat at the Battle of Tara reduced the power of the Kings of Dublin, while the murderous Battle of Clontarf in 1014 left the Irish firm masters of the island. The Scandinavians who remained developed peaceful trade, based on the towns, particularly Dublin.

Scandinavian settlement within and around the Irish Sea expanded and contracted according to the political situation within the whole area. From the early tenth century settlement areas in north-west England, northern and south-eastern Wales, were established, but reverses in one area often led people to migrate to another. In the Isle of Man, settlement began perhaps in the ninth century. Even to this day it retains its early political institutions such as the deliberative assembly, 'Tynwald', and its Speaker. The Scandinavian remains from the island are rich in carved slate cross-slabs and runic inscriptions, which suggest a very mixed population of Scandinavians and Celtic groups. The island had strong connections with Dublin and north-west England, as well as to the north.

From Norway, especially the west and south-west, there was a population movement to Iceland, far to the west by way of the Faeroes. Traditionally Iceland was discovered by accident about the year 860. It is recorded that there were Christians, probably Irish monks, living there, who left after the first Scandinavian settlers arrived. From the 870s large-scale movements began, perhaps to escape domination and oppression by Harald 'Finehair', and by the mid tenth century one estimate puts the population at fifty to sixty thousand. Vikings from Ireland, some with their native slaves and womenfolk, and groups from the Orkneys and Hebrides joined the migrations to Iceland. The colonisation and division of this empty land by the chief families is recorded in the early thirteenth-century *Íslendingabók*. While tailored to accommodate political realities of the period in which it was written, it reflects a historical tradition concerning the formation of the Icelandic Republic in 930. The island was divided into four quarters, governed by local assemblies of freemen while the supreme legislative assembly, the Althing, met every year (29).

It was to Iceland first that Eirík 'the Red' went after leaving Norway 'because of some killing'. Further trouble led to his outlawry even from this country for three years, during which he prospected the coasts of

28 *Horse-collar found at Mammen in Jutland, ornamented in the tenth-century Jellinge style.*

Greenland, a land discovered by Gunnbjörn about the year 900. On his return to Iceland Eirík could not resolve his troubles so, gathering a band of followers, who were lured perhaps by the flattering name of the new territory, he led a colonising venture there in 986. Two main focuses of settlement, known as the Western and Eastern Settlement, were established. Few remains survive from the early Viking period in Greenland, other than a few poor artefacts and foundations from turf and stone structures. From saga traditions we can name the occupiers of certain settlements: Eirík 'the Red' chose Brattahlíd, and it has been suggested that the small turf structure which has been excavated is the church erected by his wife Thjódhild. Subsistence was always difficult and supplies during a bad year had to be obtained from Iceland. The settlements survived into the later Middle Ages when they finally died out, isolated and forgotten.

Tradition has it that by being blown off course on a journey to Greenland Bjarni Herjúlfsson, discovered North America in about 985. Whether Celtic monks did first set foot there or not, it is in the Scandinavian sagas that the first incontrovertible accounts occur. Leif 'the Lucky' Eiriksson prospected the newly found territory from Greenland. He named three separate areas: Markland (forestland), now identified with Labrador; Vínland (meadowland), now North Newfoundland; and Helluland (flat stone land). Thorfinn Karlsefni settled a colony in Vínland, a land with wild corn, grapes, rich fishing and mild winters. But after trouble with the native 'skrælings' he abandoned his attempt and returned to Greenland.

A map which claims to incorporate pre-Columbus information in the delineation of the coast of north-east America, the so-called 'Vínland Map', is regarded by many scholars as a forgery. Recent analytical tests on the ink have identified a pigment not isolated and used until the twentieth century. Knowledge displayed by the map is far more closely related to exploration during the later medieval phase of the Greenland settlement than Viking journeys. Certain chance archaeological finds such as genuine Viking weapons or a recently found Scandinavian coin are of little value since the circumstances in which they were discovered and their date of arrival in America remain unsubstantiated. It is known that 'antiquities' such as the Kensington Stone with its runes are fraudulent, but archaeology, scientifically practised and scrupulously documented, does support the saga record. Incontrovertible excavated evidence comes from the settlement at L'Anse-aux-Meadows in Newfoundland, where a series of radio-carbon analyses date the site to about the year AD 1000. A bronze ring-headed pin of a type well known in Scandinavian Atlantic settlements, a soapstone spindle-whorl of normal Viking-Age type, and other artefacts make its cultural affinity certain. The structure and internal arrangements of some of the buildings can be approximately paralleled in Iceland and Greenland, and the techniques used in working local bog-iron

29 *Thingvellir, the meeting-place of the Althing, the Icelandic annual general assembly.*

69

are Scandinavian. No aspect of the site can be linked with native Indian tradition.

Doubtless there were other Viking voyages to the North American coast which are not recorded in the literature, and these perhaps resulted in ephemeral settlement, but the salient point is that the discoveries were not exploited. Although agriculturally rich and accessible by sea and inland waterways, America was at the end of a very long chain of communication. Conflict with the hostile natives proved too demoralising for the isolated immigrants, and the period of dynamic Scandinavian expansion had effectively ended by the time this New World was discovered.

In contrast to the western seaways followed by the Norwegians, the Danes were active in England, the Low Countries and France. From 835 there were almost annual raids, and after 851 armies began to winter in England. In 867 York was seized and in 876 'Halfdan shared out the land of the Northumbrians, and they proceeded to plough and support themselves'. Territory in other Anglo-Saxon kingdoms was appropriated. In 880 an army went from Cirencester into East Anglia and 'settled there and shared out the land'. After a spirited resistance, led by King Alfred the Great and based on the Anglo-Saxon kingdom of Wessex, the country was partitioned formally in 886. The Scandinavian part of England later became known as the 'Danelaw', that is, where Scandinavian customs and law were current. The area lay very broadly north and east of a line from Chester to London, and included Leicestershire, Lincolnshire, Nottinghamshire and Yorkshire which had the densest settlement. The Danes had been driven out of urban centres they had seized, such as London, but the 'Five Boroughs' of Derby, Leicester, Lincoln, Nottingham and Stamford remained in their hands, while the Kingdom of York became the main Anglo-Scandinavian trading-centre of the North Sea basin. The Anglo-Saxons began to reconquer the area in the early tenth century, but the influx of Scandinavian population added considerably to agricultural wealth and prosperity.

The written sources are silent about the number of new settlers and their relationships with the original population, which remained largely where it was. The Viking kingdom of York, Jórvík, as it was known to the Scandinavians, although finally incorporated into the English kingdom in 954, continued to be a centre of great trade and craft activities. The defences of the Roman city were re-fortified but the main commercial centre lay outside them. The Scandinavians appear to have adopted Christianity and soon became integrated with the English population. The political power of the town was based on support from the Scandinavians of the region round about. Some became landowners, taking over estates and lands as functioning taxable units. In places such as Middleton, a Yorkshire village retaining its Anglo-Saxon place-name, the parish church has a series of monuments decorated in provincial Anglo-Scandinavian style, presumably to cater for the taste of a powerful patron (30).

The Scandinavians gave names in their own language to places on the basis of topographically prominent features, or the name of the founding settler. A village or farm was often named with the element '-by', or

30 *A stone cross, showing a tenth-century Viking landowner with his warrior's equipment, from Middleton, Yorkshire.*

'-thorp': Aismunderby in Yorkshire is 'Asmund's farm'. A stream, 'bekkr', may appear, as in Caldbeck, Cumberland. A settlement of Anglo-Saxons got called Ingleby. Such names were different from those of the Anglo-Saxons, and it is possible to distinguish linguistically between places named by Norwegians and Danes. The density of place-names of Scandinavian origin may be an indicator of the density of Scandinavian settlement – in the East and North Ridings of Yorkshire up to 40 per cent of early recorded names are Scandinavian. By comparing the agricultural potential of land in areas with Anglo-Saxon place-names with that of areas with predominantly Scandinavian place-names, it can be shown that the newcomers sometimes settled poorer land. This implies that the Anglo-Saxon farmers kept under cultivation the best land, or that the newcomers did not change the place-names when they settled. In counties like Lincolnshire the field-names are heavily Scandinavian, suggesting an influx of Viking peasant cultivators who actually worked the fields.

These scraps of evidence suggest that in England the Scandinavian takeover of land was complex, and not simply brutal appropriation. It has been suggested that silver acquired by looting in England, France and elsewhere was used by men who wished to settle down in peace and purchase a plot of land in the adopted country. But when there was a general share-out of English land among an army some men who were unwilling to settle left to carry on raiding in England and across the Channel, where they resorted in force after reverses in England.

Around the coasts of northern France and Frisia in the ninth century, there were a few scattered, short-lived settlements intended especially as bases for raids inland. In Brittany the Vikings seized brief control in the tenth century. In 911 Rollo gained formal recognition from Charles 'the Simple' of his control of land which became the Duchy of Normandy. Rapidly adapting to local language and religion, the Scandinavians settled there, building a powerful state, the ruler of which in 1066 took over control of the English kingdom by invasion and conquest.

By contrast, the Swedes were mainly active eastwards, where settlements were planted from the late seventh century along the Baltic coast and beyond. The earliest, such as Grobin, included settlers from Gotland and Uppland and lay on the east Baltic coast in the territory of Baltic tribal groups. In the western Slav territory Scandinavians settled as traders in existing urban centres, where the range of activities was similar to that developing in Scandinavia (p. 48). Their characteristic burial practices can be found in small isolated cemeteries or in larger native ones. Further inland there may have been small groups of mercenaries.

For several centuries there has been heated discussion concerning the extent and effects of Scandinavian influence on the eastern Slavs in Russia. Political and economic development, particularly in regard to the formation of towns, has been ascribed by some to a Scandinavian domination and by others to internal development. Numbers of Scandinavians with their women formed groups in certain urban centres. The men acted as traders and tax-gatherers to accumulate wealth, or as mercenaries, and took political power as opportunity offered.

Burials along the great rivers and in natural centres of trade and communication sometimes contain Scandinavian objects. Where contact took place through trade the possession of Scandinavian jewellery and weapons says little about the identity of the wearer. Some burials are specialised in rite, such as near Yaroslavl, where clay representations of animal paws were found in cremation burials; these have parallels only in the Åland Islands. But it was characteristic of many Viking settlements where there was an existing population that the Scandinavians integrated with the local community and adopted the local burial rite.

From the ninth century onwards the town of Staraja Ladoga, known to the Scandinavians as Aldeigjuborg, contained material of Swedish affinity including a runic inscription. Situated on the south of Lake Ladoga, it was a focus for trade-routes along the rivers, leading to the south and east (p. 52). In the neighbouring south Ladoga region there are numerous burials containing Scandinavian objects. The situation of fortified towns containing merchant settlements and craft workshops, with a scattered Viking population outside the town, is similar to that in parts of western Europe. Novgorod, known to the Scandinavians as Hólmgardr, came traditionally under Scandinavian political control during the ninth century. At Gnezdovo near Smolensk there is evidence of a large urban complex with a great cemetery near by, where there are relatively large numbers of Scandinavian objects for male and female use.

Further south in the Middle Dniepr region lay Kiev, a great centre owing its riches to trade with Byzantium and controlling a major source of furs by taxing many of the Slavs in territories round about. There were Scandinavian traders here, and Oleg, a Scandinavian, is traditionally said to have taken over the city in 882 and begun to levy taxes systematically from the neighbouring Slav tribes. In the tenth century Scandinavians served here as mercenaries, and some scattered archaeological material may provide evidence of this. Exiles such as Harald 'the Ruthless' from Norway sometimes served there as mercenaries on the way to Byzantium and in the later Viking Age marriage connections between the Scandinavian and Kievan ruling families strengthened these links, for example, the marriage between Yaroslav the Wise and Ingigerd, the daughter of Olaf Sköttkonung.

Russia was known in Scandinavia as Gardaríki (the land of towns), and clearly the Vikings were able to dominate commercial activities here to their great advantage. But of many early Russian towns we know relatively little, because they have been continuously occupied. Although the country is so vast that information about rural settlement is sparse, it is possible that, as in Ireland, Scandinavian population was largely restricted to urban settlements.

It has been due to a series of excavations during the post-war years in many parts of the Viking world that the character and importance of Viking towns has been strikingly demonstrated. The most successful excavations have shed new light on the period by uncovering objects and structures which greatly extend our understanding of such settlements, and their relationships with the surrounding rural populace.

5 House and Home

Methods of building and types of houses varied throughout the Viking world. This was partly because settlers tended to adopt local traditions of building and partly because of the different materials available. In areas which were extensively wooded, such as Denmark, timber was the natural building material but in the treeless, exposed Atlantic islands builders were forced to use stone and turf.

Our knowledge of the Vikings' homes and the life they led within them has been transformed in recent years by modern excavations. The south Danish town of Hedeby has been more extensively explored than any other such Viking site and an extraordinary number of objects has survived. A rising water-level has waterlogged much of the original occupation deposits, excluding the air which encourages decay and preserving, not only objects of wood and leather that normally perish in the ground, but also the remains of quantities of food. Most exciting are the substantial remains of timber buildings. As the houses and workshops of Hedeby fell into disrepair, they were demolished and the site levelled before rebuilding. In one remarkable instance the walls of a house had been pushed over and left flat in the ground, until uncovered largely intact in 1968 by German archaeologists.

The permanent inhabitants of Hedeby seem to have lived around a stream which ran through the middle of the town. The gables of their houses faced on to wood-paved streets. The closely spaced plots were fenced with wattle and sometimes also contained outhouses and a well. Similar arrangements and density of occupation have been found by excavation at Dublin and York, where waterlogged levels have also conserved the remains of timber houses.

The commonest building technique at Hedeby was stave-construction, in which tree-trunks are split lengthwise and placed vertically in the ground to form a continuous wall. Wattle houses were plastered with mud or dung. The roofs at Hedeby were thatched with reeds, or covered with turves, but the use of wooden shingles for roofing has been discovered at Trelleborg. Some of the smaller Hedeby houses, as elsewhere in Denmark, had sunken floors. In York similar structures lined with horizontal planks have recently been excavated (31).

On the evidence recovered at Hedeby it has been possible to reconstruct an accurate full-size town house with walls of wattle and daub. There are no load-bearing posts within the house, so buttresses are used to prevent the walls splaying out under the weight of the roof. In plan the house measures about sixteen by forty feet and is divided into rooms (fig. 4). One of the outer rooms contained a clay bread-oven, the size of which suggests

31 *Viking York: row of tenth-century workshops or storehouses, under excavation in Coppergate.*

75

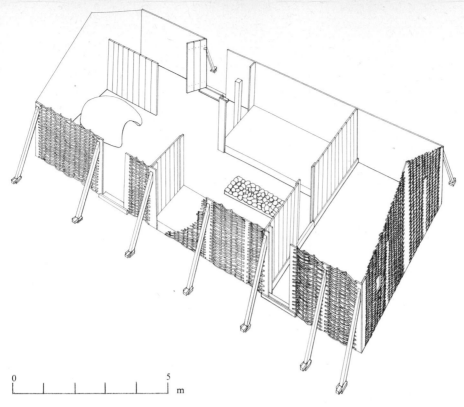

Fig. 4 LEFT *Isometric reconstruction of a ninth-century house based on excavations at Hedeby.*

32 BELOW *Interior of the Hedeby house as reconstructed at Moesgård, Denmark.*

0   5
          m

that the occupants may even have been professional bakers; the room at the opposite end of the house is of unknown use. The living-room lies between these two and has a central hearth made of stones topped with clay (32). On either side of it low earth platforms have been built up to act as benches for sitting and sleeping, although in this case a wooden bed has been added, based on one found in the Oseberg ship-burial. The loom stands ready for use against the opposite wall, while the cooking-pot hangs over the hearth, which provides both heat and light in this windowless house. More light would enter through the hole in the roof provided for the smoke to escape, but any detailed work would have been done outside, or by lamp-light. Lamps were small bowls for burning oil and could be made of iron, in which case they might have a spike for sticking into the floor, or of soapstone, sometimes with suspension loops; pottery lamps were being made at Hedeby and might have been used in such a house as this.

There were larger houses at Hedeby, with up to about a thousand square feet of floor space, but even more impressive in the Danish landscape would have been the late tenth-century houses of the Viking ring-forts (p. 124). The Trelleborg house, named after those in the most famous of the forts, was built of timber. Its long walls were curved, producing a curved roof-ridge and giving it a 'hog-backed' appearance. The Trelleborg houses were stave-built and had buttresses; some were entered through porches, one on each side, at opposite ends of the long walls. Inside they were divided into three rooms, the central one being the largest, with a hearth and benches in the case of dwelling-houses.

A Trelleborg-type house was among those excavated at the Jutland village of Lindholm Høje (50), and further examples have been turning up during recent investigations of even larger Danish villages, also of late Viking-Age date. But at Lindholm Høje there were in addition other types of houses, including long rectangular houses and huts with sunken floors, like those discovered at Hedeby. The most unusual was a square house with a courtyard – a type that only became common at a somewhat later date.

In the Viking settlements on the Atlantic islands houses were built in drystone, or in a mixture of turf and stone, or even in turf alone (although this was placed on stone foundations). Such walls were massive in construction, up to six feet thick, so that no external buttresses were required; additional roof-support if needed was provided by two rows of internal posts. The first Norse settlers at Jarlshof, at the southern tip of Shetland, built themselves a farmstead in this manner in the ninth century. The chief building was a seventy-foot-long, two-roomed dwelling-house, with curved sides. Associated with it were the necessary outhouses for a farm, including a barn, a byre and a small smithy, and also what seems to have been a small bath-house, containing a hearth for a steam-bath or sauna. As the settlement expanded, so extra dwelling-houses were added to the original group to cope with the increased population.

Such arrangements seem to have been typical of the first settlements in the Atlantic islands. For instance, a similar house with a barn has been excavated at Kvívík in the Faeroes, with walls of turf on stone. The first farms built in Iceland were of this type, but the settlers there soon modified the basic hall-house and developed more complex buildings with several smaller rooms. This new type of farmhouse is known particularly well from a series of excavations carried out in a southern Icelandic valley, devastated by an eruption of the volcano Hekla in about 1104. The sites that were in use then were smothered in volcanic ash and had to be abandoned. They were all of the same general type, so that the one at Stöng may be taken as representative of late Viking-Age farms in Iceland. Its excavated plan has recently been used as a basis for a full-size reconstruction, in Iceland (33), of such an eleventh-century farmhouse.

As can be seen from its plan (fig. 5), the house at Stöng was entered by a single door, leading into a vestibule attached to the main hall, identified by its large central hearth and broad benches. The turf walls were lined with panelling, but with an air-gap left between the two. A smaller living-room led off one end of the hall, with a small box-like fireplace and narrow benches round the walls, only suitable for sitting on and not for sleeping; it housed the loom. Also opening off the hall (but at right angles to it) was a dairy, with space for three large vats. Off the vestibule was another, but smaller, back-room with a drainage channel down either side, suggesting that it was a lavatory. Outhouses consisted of a byre, a store and a smithy.

Fig. 5 BELOW *Plan of a turf-built Icelandic farmhouse at Stöng, as it was when destroyed by a volcanic eruption in about 1104, and* 33 RIGHT *a reconstruction based upon it.*

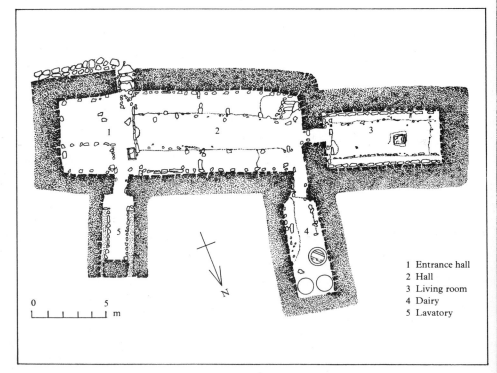

0   5   m

1 Entrance hall
2 Hall
3 Living room
4 Dairy
5 Lavatory

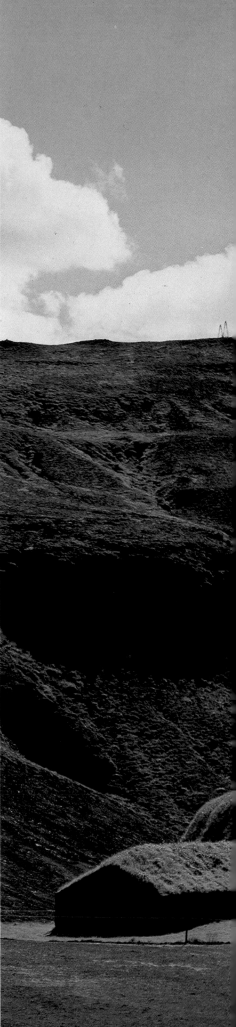

The furnishings of all these houses would have been simple, with the fixed benches used for both sitting and sleeping. Tables and shelves (but not cupboards) have been found, and also portable chairs and simple stools. An ornamented plank appears to be from some more elaborate piece of furniture. Decorated bedheads belonging to free-standing beds are known from the rich ship-burials, but these may have been intended only for the use of wealthy travellers. Clothes and personal possessions would have been kept in chests (like those of the Oseberg burial), or hung on hooks. Food was stored in wooden vats and tubs, in large soapstone bowls, or in pots (34). Little attention was paid to floors, which would have been of stamped earth, perhaps strewn with reeds or straw. But interior walls, if panelled, might be carved or painted, or even decorated with woven hangings.

The central hearth was the focal point of the house, providing not only heat and light, but also the stove for cooking. A cauldron was suspended over it for making porridge and soups, or for stewing meat. The finest and most substantial of these cauldrons were made of iron (35); but soapstone bowls with iron handles were also used. Meat was roasted on spits (72), or long forks, and iron grill-pans and griddles were also used. Alternatively,

34 BELOW *Clay pots and wooden utensils excavated in Lund.*

35 RIGHT *An iron cauldron from Sweden.*

meat and fish were baked in holes in the ground, packed around with heated stones. Food was eaten with a knife from a wooden trencher, or with a spoon from a bowl (34). Wooden cups were used for drinking (34), although horns were also used (with occasionally imported glasses for wine).

The diet of many Vikings was varied and nourishing. Meat and fish were dried or preserved in a number of ways, or eaten raw. Wild fruits and vegetables supplemented the cultivated peas, beans and cabbage. They ate bread made from barley or rye and porridge made from oats and barley; grain was also important for brewing beer. Honey was the base for fermenting mead, but the strongest drink available to the Vikings was home-made wine from fermented fruit juices. True wine was certainly imported but would have been consumed only by the wealthiest. Milk would also have been drunk and all forms of dairy produce were an important part of the diet. For those with few resources, however, the diet must have been much less varied and particularly monotonous during harsh seasons.

Cooking and brewing were, of course, a principal task of the Viking women but they also had many other jobs, including spinning and weaving. Much of the cloth they produced would have been for family clothing but a great deal was also required for sail-making, tents, awnings, wagon-covers and the like, including wall-hangings. Spindle-whorls of many different materials are among the commonest of all archaeological finds and the spinning of wool may well have been a communal task. But first the shorn or plucked wool would have been cleaned and combed. The spun yarn was wound into balls, or into skeins if it was to be dyed.

The wool was woven (as was linen) on an upright loom, leant against the wall. This, with warps weighted at the bottom by stone or baked-clay weights, was no different from the modern primitive loom. The skein, or ball, of wool was passed from side to side without the aid of a shuttle, the weft being straightened with a weaving batten – a sword-like object of wood, whalebone or even iron. Detailed adjustments were made with the aid of special weaving-combs and small pointed tools (pin-beaters) of wood or bone. Other forms of textile work included tablet-weaving, for producing ornamental borders and braids, and embroidery.

There was also sewing, mending and washing to be done. The large whalebone plaques, sometimes found in women's graves, may have been used as a form of ironing-board, with bun-shaped smoothers of glass. These plaques seem to have been quite prestigious objects since they often have finely ornamented tops (36). They could have been used for smoothing linen, or maybe for pleating it, by folding and winding it round the board while it was still wet, and then leaving it to dry.

Feasting was an important part of the life of the Viking community. Ale-feasts celebrated religious festivals and with the coming of Christianity the Vikings were unwilling to relinquish these and carried them over into their new religion. Such occasions served to strengthen bonds of kinship, as well as relieving some of the tedium of long northern winters. The hangovers would have been most debilitating, given the impurities contained in their

36 *Whalebone plaque from northern Norway, ornamented with animal heads.*

drink! But, as always, this never stopped a man boasting of his drinking prowess. 'I leave no ale in the horn, though the warrior brings me the horn till morning' was the claim of Egill Skalla-grímsson, as distinguished a poet as he was a Viking.

Poetry, games and entertainments undoubtedly accompanied feasts, but such relaxations and pastimes were not confined to these occasions. Little is known of Viking music, although a few remains of stringed instruments and pipes have been found. On the other hand there is much evidence for board-games, even if it is not always clear what sort of game was being played. Pieces were made of bone, amber or glass (37); one common type of game used sixteen pieces of one colour against eight pieces and a 'king' of another. The Baldursheimur bone figure from Iceland (38) is such a 'king', and was associated with twenty-four gaming-pieces, forming a set of so-called *hneftafl*. The best-preserved gaming-board to survive was made in the tenth century in some Viking settlement, though found on a native Irish site, at Ballinderry (39). This is for an old form of the modern game of 'Fox and Geese'. Chess may have been known in Scandinavia by the end of the Viking Age.

Outdoor pastimes in the winter would have been restricted, but skating and ball-games on the ice were enjoyed. In the summer, as well as boating, swimming, fishing and practising with weapons, there were thrilling sports like horse-racing and horse-fighting where the spectators might be as much in danger as the competitors.

Even the Scandinavians who stayed at home lived lives full of incident and hazard, threatened by pirates, warring neighbours and family feud. 'Let the man who opens a door be on the lookout for an enemy behind it' was the poet's warning in *Hávamál*, a poem of Viking Age origin. Valour was certainly not the ultimate Viking virtue, for at bottom it was the family and home life that mattered the most. Those who wanted to stay alive combined caution with their bravery. In *Hávamál* we are told: 'Praise not the day until evening has come; a woman until she is burnt; a sword until it is tried; a maiden until she is married; ice until it has been crossed; beer until it has been drunk'.

37 LEFT *Glass gaming-pieces from the rich cemetery at Valsgärde in Sweden.*

38 OPPOSITE TOP LEFT *Whalebone 'king' from an Icelandic board-game.*

39 OPPOSITE *A tenth-century wooden gaming-board from Ireland.*

6 Death and Pagan Gods

The early Vikings were pagans – they had not yet been converted to a belief in Christianity. They acknowledged many gods and spirits who might be invoked in different situations, according to their varying powers. For some, Christ was one god tolerated among many others. Their looting of churches and monasteries and seizing of plate, vestments and valuables was not the result of organised, anti-Christian feelings, but appropriation from a rich source of wealth protected by a ritual sanction they did not recognise. Unlike the Christian Church, Viking religion did not support the secular state in a formal way, although many chiefs had a religious function as intermediary with the gods.

When Christianity was imposed on the Vikings, the Church pursued a deliberate policy of destroying material and beliefs associated with pagan observances. Some information we have about these beliefs comes down through largely hostile contemporary observers. Sources such as the Icelandic sagas contain much information on myths and legends current in thirteenth-century Iceland, but the Vikings' original beliefs may have become much altered. The accounts of both Arab and Christian sources may have been distorted by a tendency to explain what they heard in terms of their own practices. In any case, the corpus of Viking beliefs about death and deities was the result of many centuries of complex development, influenced from many sources.

Contemporary representations of gods and mythical scenes exist, and it is possible to interpret some of them from fragmentary accounts available to us. These range from legends about the creation of the universe, through to the predestined destruction of the old order of the gods: Ragnarök – the end of the world. Within this complex were stories of dwarves and giants and monsters of evil, against which the gods were constantly in combat. Myths of the mighty gods emphasised that they were often human in their appetites and foibles, even if superhuman in their excesses. And they did walk abroad, influencing affairs in the world.

Among statuettes which survive, some figures are easily identifiable by the way that certain features are emphasised. The god of fertility, Freyr, was important for agricultural communities who depended on the growing of crops and breeding of herds. He can be seen with long virile beard and pointed cap, sitting with his phallus erect (40). The long beard is a clue to the identification of an ivory statuette from Lund which may also represent Freyr, although an identification with Thor is also possible. A series of rectangular gold plaques may show Freyr and the giantess Gerd represented as a couple in various ritual embraces (41). What purpose these delicate sheets served is uncertain. In a society where marriage was

40 LEFT *Bronze statuette of Freyr, the god of fertility, from Rällinge, Sweden.*

41 FAR LEFT ABOVE AND CENTRE *Sheet-gold plaques with the embracing figures of the god Freyr and the giantess Gerd, from Hauge, Norway.*

42 FAR LEFT BELOW *A silver pendant, perhaps a protective amulet, from Aska, Sweden.*

arranged for the young by their elders, and where love played no part in the initial arrangements, fertility was the test of a successful union; perhaps good-luck charms were needed to ensure this.

The use of amulets or charms, for whatever reason, was popular among the Vikings, both men and women. The identities behind the grimly-moustached human masks set on certain silver pendants are no longer known (42), but they may have acted as protection. Equally enigmatic is a series of small female figures, often delicately rendered to show details of their modish garments and coiffured hair. One with a drinking-horn (43) probably represents a Valkyrie. These maidens, according to one legend, rode in the sky over fields of battle as attendants of the god of war. In another tradition the Valkyries served at Valhalla where the souls of brave warriors who died in battle feasted, drank and fought.

Thor, the strongest and most popular of the gods, may have afforded protection to those wearing amulets in the form of the hammer. His famous battle hammer, Mjöllnir, was a powerful weapon in the fight of the gods against the powers of evil that constantly threatened to overwhelm them. On the example from Bredsätra the mask of a fierce animal broods over the end of the handle, perhaps a guardian spirit (44), while the handle of the hammer from Foss terminates in a fierce dragon-head (45). It was a

belief in the protective power of amulets which may explain the shaping of the broad battle-axe and the cross at the heads of some dress-pins found at Jarlshof. Amber pendants (74) from Hedeby in the form of an axe may have the same significance, and so may the silver miniatures – sword, spear, fire-steel and staves – on a small ring from Klinta.

For the Vikings, the creatures and beings of the other world were not so compartmentalised as they are for us. The world was constantly threatened by demons and monsters, unseen but still lurking, who were destined to destroy the world. These, with lesser deities and local spirits were forces to be reckoned with. It is not difficult to see the animal ornament on everyday objects as an expression of this world view, and in studying the more elaborate pieces we may imagine stories being told around the fire about the creatures who form the designs.

Even on the most functional of objects decoration may have a symbolic significance. A soapstone furnace-stone from Snaptun is strongly incised with a face-mask displaying prominent eyebrows and a moustache. The lips are disfigured with lines across them which may represent stitches (46). This may be a representation of the god Loki, who caused so much dissension among the gods by his destructive jealousy and spite. Having once wagered his head against that of Brokk the dwarf, and being about to

43 LEFT *Silver toilet implement from Birka, bearing a female figure, perhaps a valkyrie.*

44 FAR LEFT AND CENTRE LEFT *Silver pendants in the form of a Thor's hammer from Bredsätra, Sweden, and Rømersdal, Denmark.*

45 ABOVE *Silver pendant in the form of a cross with a dragon's head terminal, from Foss, Iceland.*

46 RIGHT *Furnace-stone to protect a bellows-nozzle, incised with the face of the god Loki, from Snaptun, Denmark.*

lose it, he saved himself by pointing out there had been no mention of his neck in the bet! Enraged, the dwarves sewed his lips together. And since later tradition accords Loki the position of a fire-being of the hearth, it is appropriate that this object would have been in the heat of the forge.

On Gotland was a long series of painted memorial stones with a variety of figural scenes, some of them involving complex narrative. While they must have had significance for contemporary viewers, not all the scenes are comprehensible to us. The stone from Smiss (8) depicts a ship full of armed warriors, and a single combat between two swordsmen. This may record an actual event, which led to the death of the man commemorated by the monument, or may be a mythical scene.

An early Viking-Age stone from Lillbjärs shows a mounted warrior with conical helmet and pantaloon breeches, bearing an emblazoned shield (47). He is met by a woman offering a horn of drink. This may be the representation of the dead man riding from a field of battle to Valhalla where he is met by a ministering Valkyrie. Those who fell in combat were reputed to travel direct to this drinking-hall of the heroes, where they remained in readiness until called upon by Odin to fight alongside the gods at the end of the world. Below this, two mysterious cloaked figures with jutting beards sail their lonely ship. One has control of the rudder while the other appears to be a passenger – perhaps the dead passing over to the spirit world. But who is it who stands alone, bearded, and with arm outstretched towards someone or something not visible to us? All round the border is a continuous running motif which echoes the interwoven triangles in the main field, commonly found in scenes of mystery.

Panels on the eleventh-century grave cist found at Ardre are decorated with scenes from myth but it is not certain if they are all related. What story lies behind the appearance of a figure, who is armed prominently with a sword and standing hemmed in at the centre of a scene dominated by monsters (48)? On a fragmentary panel can be seen an eight-legged horse ridden by an armed man, perhaps Odin riding his wind-swift steed, Sleipnir. Above is a swordsman carrying a great spear in one hand, and putting a horn to his mouth to sound a warning, as the watchman Heimdall was to do at the end of the world. On one side-panel, a god-like figure is seen between two long-necked, four-legged monsters. He is entwined in mortal combat with a long serpent, aided perhaps by a lesser figure behind him, while a free figure at the bottom of the scene is gripping the body of one serpent. This may be yet another representation of the end of the world.

From Andreas on the Isle of Man a fragment of carved slate, part of a tenth-century Christian monument, bears a detail from identifiable legend (49). Originally the surface had carved on it a tall cross, with down its shaft a typically Viking decorative motif, the ring-chain. Under one arm of the cross stands Odin, one of the mightiest gods and the most mysterious. His harbinging, all-seeing raven perches on his shoulder. Odin strikes downwards with his spear at Fenrir, the wolf, who gnaws at his leg, and who is predestined to devour him. For when the world inevitably ends with Ragnarök, the destruction of the gods by ill-begotten creatures of

47 *An early Viking memorial stone from Lillbjärs on Gotland.*
(The paint is modern.)

48 FAR LEFT *Panels of a stone cist carved in the eleventh-century Urnes style, from Ardre, Gotland.*

49 LEFT *Odin devoured by the Fenrir wolf on a fragment of a stone monument from Andreas, Isle of Man.*

evil, that is to be his immutable fate. On the reverse of the fragment is a figure grasping a Christian processional cross and a book. He tramples upon a gigantic serpent while at his feet is a fish, a Christian symbol. He is a token of the new spiritual order which, more than the monsters of dark places, was to destroy the fastness of the gods. In areas where there was already a population of Christians, such as the Isle of Man or northern England, there grew up a fusion of pagan and Christian iconographies, characteristic of the eclectic nature of Viking taste.

In contrast to the later Christian practice of burial in hallowed ground often around a church, pagan cemeteries were close to the settlements they served. Small, rural burial-grounds often lay in sight of the homefield as a group of low mounds on a patch of poor agricultural land. At Birka the cemeteries lay close to the concentration of houses, beyond the rampart which was constructed later. The size of the cemetery (over three thousand graves) indicates the population and wealth of the town.

The simplest graves consisted of a hole in the ground, sometimes with a coffin or hollowed-out tree-trunk and covered over with a low mound. There seems to have been some belief that the dead resided in the place they were buried. It was the pagan practice to bury women in costume with their jewellery, or men with weapons or tools. Each might have treasured possessions and items showing their role and status in the stratified Viking society. The poor had nothing. The practice suggests some belief in an after-life, while the deposition of food may be seen as token sustenance for the journey. The unburnt body buried in the ground is, therefore, our richest source of information about the Vikings, until Christianity put an end to the practice of depositing such accessories. Some of the richest graves may have been looted soon after burial by those who knew what wealth was contained in them. Large, carefully built wooden chambers were sometimes constructed for such burials. The sword from Hedeby (83) was beside a man placed in such a chamber and buried under the middle part of a ship. The Viking tradition of burying the powerful in a boat, or under a ship-shaped stone-setting, is of great antiquity in Scandinavia. It may reflect the status of the dead as captain and owner, and also the mode of journey to the other world. Women too were accorded splendid burials, such as the great barge in a mound at Oseberg, while in Jutland others appear to have been buried in the body of a wagon. The owner of the rich jewellery from a chamber-grave at Birka (56) was buried with a range of rich imports like other powerful figures.

Slave-owning was a privilege of the more powerful, and slaves could be treated as chattels to be disposed of as the master pleased. The Arab traveller Ibn Fadlan records, in the early tenth century, the ritual sacrifice of a slave-girl on the banks of the Volga to accompany her dead Viking master. In the British Isles, this practice is borne out by the discovery of the body of a woman from a burial-mound at Ballateare in the Isle of Man, placed in a position secondary to that of a man. The evidence from her skull shows that her young life was cut short by a sharp blow, perhaps from a sword.

Some burials lay under great artificial mounds which changed the landscape and acted as a memorial. Sometimes those who died abroad or in battle were commemorated by their family or comrades on memorial stones: 'and they lie in London' like two men from Valleberga in southern Sweden. Of one leader, Toke, we learn that 'He fled not at Uppsala, but fought while he had weapons'.

Some groups in Scandinavia still adhered to the old rite of cremation where the body was burnt on a pyre. An Arab source records that this step released the soul to fly to 'paradise', whatever that might mean. Some burnt, calcined bones with charcoal and ash might be put in a simple clay vessel and buried, or a low mound might be raised over a patch of charcoal from the pyre. Stone settings in different shapes sometimes marked the grave, as at Lindholm Høje (50). Fragments of costume jewellery or possessions burnt with the dead might be included, giving the only clue to the period of burial. Prized possessions might first have been smashed or mutilated so as to be useless, like the 'killed' sword from Wallstena. The Christian Church forbade the cremating of the dead as an irreconcilably pagan practice.

The Christian Church also forbade the pagan rites and celebrations which accompanied the burial of the dead. These have left little or no physical traces, and our knowledge of them rests on contemporary sources. People who officiated at the burial ceremonies did so by virtue of their age and experience, as much as from religious authority. While we know that Viking chieftains had a religious role, there is only one late reference to an organised priesthood, in Sweden. In the accounts of foreign writers there are rare references to pagan temples in Scandinavia, while in a few Viking place-names there is the suggestion of a religious site: in Iceland, for example, the element 'hof' implies a building for pagan worship. No positive identifications of a temple have yet been made from the archaeological finds, but since these consist only of ground-plans, a normal timber building devoted to pagan practices might not be identifiable. Lejre on Sjælland in Denmark, and Old Uppsala in Sweden are mentioned as religious centres, and have been traditionally important. Instead of there being a formal religious structure, it is possible that natural features like a grim old tree or boulder were venerated. Weapons, especially swords, have often been found in rivers, which may have been places for sacrifice, but other explanations are possible for these occurrences. Human and animal sacrifice to the gods are occasionally mentioned in connection with pagan rites by Christian and Arab authorities. In Iceland the ritual feasting upon horseflesh was ostensibly pagan, and after the proclamation of Christianity could only be done in private until it was outlawed. The burial of a horse beside the dead may relate to its religious connotations of strength and fertility as well as being a symbol of power and wealth.

Connected with both religious expression and memorials to the dead are runic inscriptions, although these also occur on simple objects to record ownership (12 and p. 34). The runic alphabet is known as the 'Futhark' from the values of its first six symbols. Their over-all shapes are unmistakable, being ideal for incising or carving and for painting. One

50 OVERLEAF *A view over the Viking cemetery at Lindholm Høje, northern Jutland; across its stone grave-markers can be seen the Limfjord.*

such alphabet is inscribed on a rib-bone from Lund (51). There are localised versions of the runic alphabet, and variations in the number of symbols and their sound-values. In some cases, there is considerable doubt about the reading and meaning of short inscriptions. Runes were a form of writing common to the Germanic tribes and used in Scandinavia from the first centuries after the birth of Christ. In the later Viking period, we read of specialist 'rune-masters'. Runes were gradually superseded from the late eleventh century by the Roman alphabet which spread with Christianity, but they remained in use to the later medieval period.

The association of runes with the mystic is explained in the poetic myth of their discovery by Odin, who hanged himself for nine nights on an ash tree to gain the secret of wisdom. He became the god of magic. And, of course, secret charms or curses would be scratched in runes. A fragment of human skull from Ribe is incised with an eighth-century inscription which today cannot be interpreted, apart from the reading of some names including that of Odin himself. But many runic inscriptions record purely everyday or public information, and this more general use begins with the Viking period. A mid-eleventh-century Danish coin of Sven Estridsson has its inscription in runic characters (68h). The most famous graffito is probably that carved on the shoulder of a majestic marble lion, originally in the Piraeus harbour of Athens, by a visiting Swede, perhaps in Byzantine service. From Hedeby comes a four-sided stave with runes on two of them. The meaning cannot be satisfactorily read but appears to be in the form of a message, a letter one might almost say, dealing with an everyday matter. The memorial cross fragment from Andreas (49), with its wealth of carving has the name of its carver Thorvald recorded along the side for all who could read it. On another carved masterpiece from St Paul's Churchyard, we read in runes that 'Ginne had the stone laid and Toke . . .' but the remainder is lost (101).

In the later Viking period, particularly in Denmark and in eastern Sweden, there is a series of stone monuments inscribed with runes. Some are grave- or memorial-stones, some are boundary-markers, others mark fords. They often record events, travels and family relationships of the people who lived there. It was inevitable with the extensive use of stone memorials and graveyard monuments in Christian contexts, that runes should be employed extensively in the late Viking period. One of the earliest Christian Viking monuments from Ardre in Gotland has a runic inscription with a Christian sentiment despite its pagan iconography: 'The sons of Liknat have raised a good monument to the memory of Ailikn, good wife, mother of Aivat, Ottar and Gairvat and Liknvi. May God and God's mother be merciful to her and to those who raised the monument the largest to be seen in Garda . . .' (48). These inscriptions and figural representations give us a tantalising glimpse of people whose names we know, but unfortunately they provide us with all too little historical information about them and their way of life.

51 *Rib-bone from Lund incised with the runic alphabet – the futhark.*

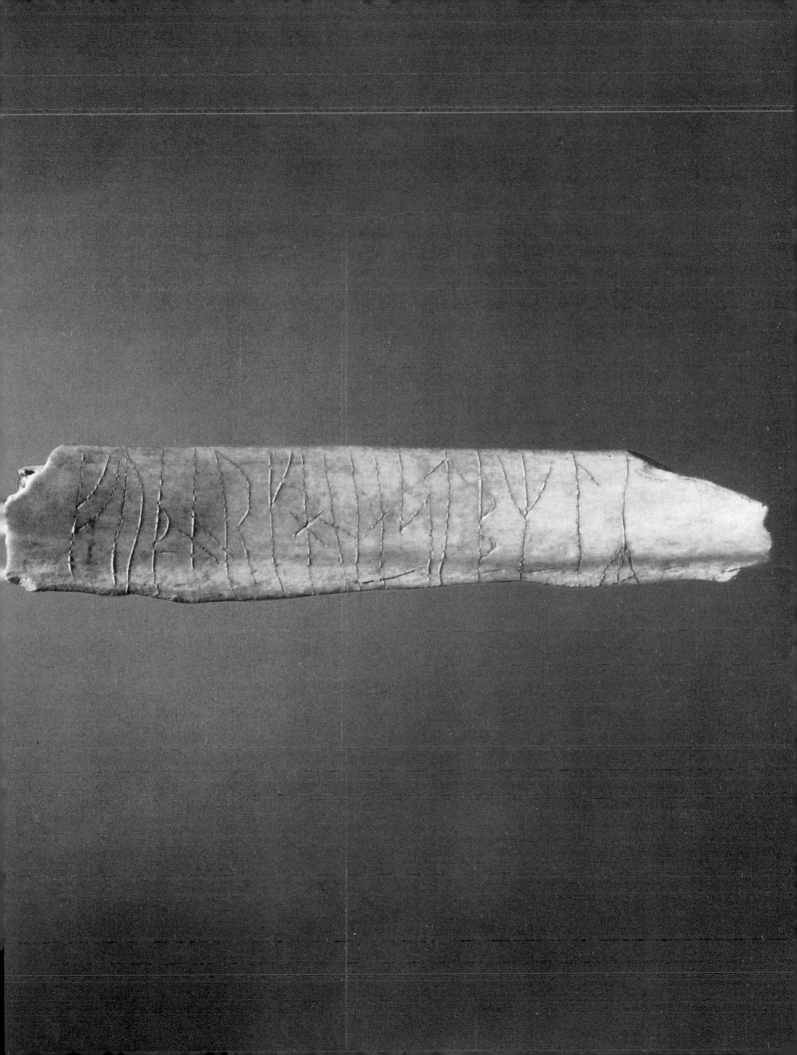

7 Viking Dress

The dress and personal equipment of the Vikings was used to display their wealth, for riches were the measure of status and success. Their love of ostentatious display is revealed in the lavish goods found in pagan burials and by the many ornaments buried in silver hoards. Ibn Fadlan described a party of northern merchants whom he met on the River Volga:

> Each woman carries on her bosom a container made of iron, silver, copper, or gold – its size and substance depending on her man's wealth. Attached to the container is a ring carrying her knife which is also tied to her bosom. Round her neck she wears gold or silver rings; when a man amasses 10,000 *dirhems* [Arabic coins] he makes his wife one gold ring; when he has 20,000 he makes two; and so the woman gets a new ring for every 10,000 *dirhems* her husband acquires, and often a woman has many of these rings.

What Ibn Fadlan does not tell us is that Viking men themselves liked to wear such rings, and fine cloak-pins and brooches of gold and silver. Indeed, the giving of rings was a traditional method by which a king rewarded his retainers. Scandinavian poets of the Viking Age, in their roundabout way, often praised their lords for hostility to gold – in other words, for their generosity, for it was considered to be their duty to distribute gold rather than to hoard it up.

Although the rich and successful could afford to wear rings and brooches of precious metal, there will have been many freemen who would have had to be content with ornaments of bronze for themselves and their wives. But even these were gilt or tinned to imitate the finery of the rich who drew their fashions from both east and west.

To reconstruct Scandinavian Viking-Age dress there are a variety of sources to which we can turn, but none is as full or reliable as we might wish. Medieval sagas provide the most extensive information, but current fashions may have affected their descriptions of the dress worn by their Viking-Age characters. Men and women are portrayed on the Gotlandic 'picture-stones' (8, 47), on the Oseberg tapestry, and in several miniatures (41, 43); little detail is shown, but the general nature of their dress emerges. Much can also be learnt from the study of grave-goods, particularly when the body was buried fully clothed. Even though the actual garments have perished in the ground, impressions of textiles may be preserved in the corrosion formed on the brooches that once held them together. Detailed study of such traces and surviving fragments of cloth have revealed much information, particularly of female dress, to expand considerably what can be learnt from contemporary pictures. But the *52 Brooches for a Viking* gradual abandonment of the pagan practice of burying grave-goods means *woman.* we are less able to follow changes in costume during the late Viking Age.

Viking settlers or traders in populated lands often adopted local dress quite rapidly as part of the process of assimilation – or simply because it was better for business. Nevertheless, there was a remarkable degree of standardisation and conservatism in the dress of Scandinavian women. It is a folk-costume that is readily recognisable to archaeology wherever the Vikings settled in the ninth and tenth centuries from the distinctive brooches that formed an essential part of it. The brooches do, however, change in detail as time passes so as to keep up with the latest style.

Viking women wore a long, sometimes trailing, garment of linen – a shift or chemise – often finely pleated and with short sleeves, or no sleeves at all. It was closed at the neck by ribbons or a drawstring (buttons and hooks were not used). Over this was a woollen tunic held up by a matched pair of bronze brooches, oval-shaped and four to five inches long (52). These oval brooches were worn high on the chest to secure the loops or shoulder-straps of the outer garment, which might be of fine and even ornamented cloth. There is no evidence that women wore belts, so that it will have hung straight, reaching nearly to the ground, or even trailing behind, as can be seen from several representations of female figures (43).

The bronze oval brooches had hollow convex shells, with the pin fitted inside so that the dress-loops would have been concealed in use. The brooches are usually well made and can be very ornate (53), but most are rather crudely ornamented in standard patterns, indicating mass-production. In fact they get cruder and uglier as the Viking Age passes, suggesting that they were of declining importance, until they were abandoned altogether by the end of the period. This trend might have been caused by a growing fashion for wearing shawls, which would of course have covered up such brooches when worn so high on the chest.

Between the oval brooches would be strung festoons of beads – of silver, amber, crystal or carnelian, but most often of multi-coloured glass (76). Elaborate necklaces are also known (55), which might be further embellished by the addition of pendants of many types (55, 54), including those of both pagan and Christian significance (45, 109). A number of personal objects could be suspended from one of the oval brooches on a chain – a knife, key, comb, toilet implements (43), small shears, or needles in a case – bringing to mind Ibn Fadlan's description quoted above.

The use of a shawl required a third brooch to hold it in place, worn in a prominent position on the middle of the chest (52). These brooches took many forms during the Viking Age from round to oblong, or even in the shape of stylised animals (103). They could be a single disc of cast silver or bronze (102), or highly elaborate, composite objects of great value and prestige (85). Common types of brooch have two symmetrical arms, or are three-lobed (56, 52), both shapes that were originally inspired by Frankish fashions. Other women proudly displayed an imported ornament as their shawl-brooch, maybe converted from a piece of loot (11), so advertising their men's success in ventures overseas.

The great majority of Scandinavian women clearly conformed to the fashion for oval brooches, except for the ladies of Gotland who preferred smaller ones shaped like animal-heads. Their jewellers had also designed

Fig. 6 *Viking dress reconstructed.*

53 LEFT *Exuberant animals
ornament a Norwegian oval
brooch.*

54 RIGHT *Pendant from
Gotland with gold filigree
ornament.*

55 *A selection of glittering and colourful necklaces for the rich, from Sweden.*

and perfected cylindrical, box-like brooches (recalling Ibn Fadlan once again) to clasp their shawls or cloaks (85). Occasionally, however, a woman of distinction took an independent line in these matters, like one lady buried at Birka with jewellery that included a pair of German enamelled brooches (replacing her oval ones), a magnificent gilt-bronze shawl-brooch, and a pair of silver-gilt, horse-shaped mounts that would have been threaded on to her necklace or sewn to her dress (56).

The simple disc-shaped brooch comes in all shapes and sizes; some were mass-produced in bronze or pewter, but others were hand-crafted, individual masterpieces in silver or gold (57). The largest of these brooches will have been used on cloaks and may well have been designed for use by men. All these brooches worn by Scandinavian men and women were generally covered with patterns of stylised animals in the changing styles of Viking art, described and illustrated in Chapter 11.

Additional ornaments were a matter of individual choice and family fortune, but finger-rings, arm-rings and neck-rings were worn by men and women alike. They form the principal ornaments that make up many of the hoards of silver and gold (18). The largest neck-ring known from the Viking Age was ploughed up at Tissø in Denmark as recently as 1977 and weighs about 4 lb of pure gold (58). It is so large and heavy, with a diameter

56 BELOW *The rich and varied ornaments buried with a lady of Birka.*

57 RIGHT *Danish gold: disc-brooches of exceptional splendour from the Hornelund hoard.*

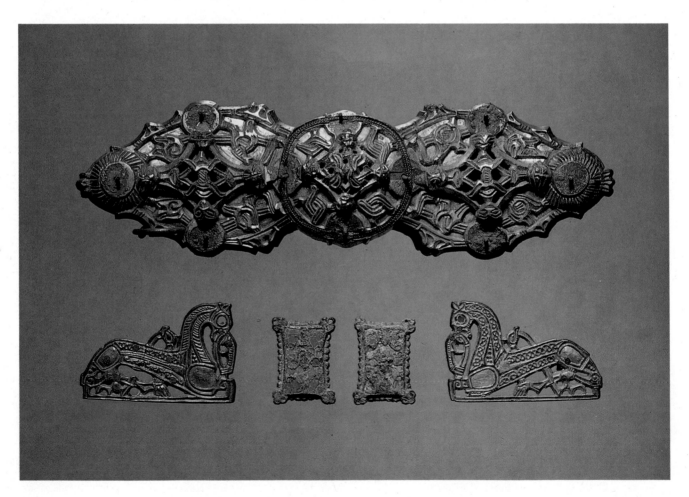

of fourteen inches, that it could only have been worn by a man – and a very stout one at that!

These rings were characteristically made of gold or silver rods that were twisted or plaited together (59), but arm-rings were also made from broad bands of silver, frequently embellished with stamped ornament. Once again those from the independently minded (and extremely wealthy) island of Gotland have their own special characteristics and design.

In winter heavy cloaks and furs were worn which would have been tied by thongs, but some brooches are so large as to suggest that they were intended expressly for garments of such thickness – not forgetting the extra opportunities so presented for display. Such a brooch as that from Møllerløkken in Denmark (60) is very practical for such a purpose. Its long, sharp pin would have pierced the thickest and toughest cloak, and a great mass of material could be bunched within its broad ring. But then its delicate gold ornaments suggest that it was only used on special occasions – feast-days, for instance.

The Møllerløkken brooch represents a particularly elaborate example of a brooch fashionable among Scandinavian men in the tenth century, but of a form which was originally adapted from brooches produced by native Irish jewellers in the late ninth century. Such western brooches and cloak-pins, which were both practical and ornate, proved immensely popular when introduced into Scandinavia, where they were imitated and elaborated. They were generally worn on the right shoulder, so that the cloak parted on that side, enabling a man to keep his sword-arm free.

Vikings with wealth to spare were most certainly fashion conscious in their dress and ornaments, the men as much as the women. Indeed, male costume was more varied and often more luxuriously trimmed than that of their women. At Birka, it was the men's graves that produced most of the imported silks and multi-coloured braids and bands, with which their tunics and cloaks were edged.

58 LEFT *Treasure from Tissø: the most massive gold neck-ring from the Viking Age.*

59 BELOW *Danish arm-rings of gold and silver.*

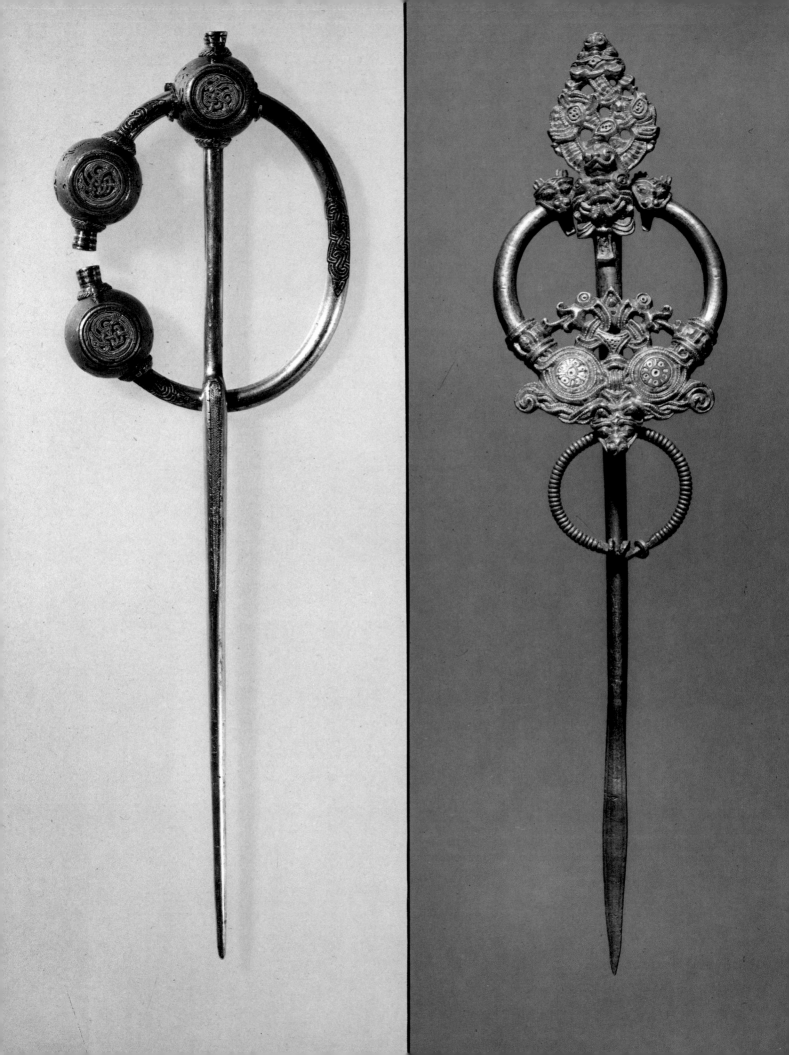

Contemporary pictures of Scandinavian men show a choice of trouser styles, presumably held up by a drawstring or sash. Some were tapered, others were worn straight, or even enormously baggy like those of the fighting warriors on the Smiss stone (8). The rider on the Lillbjärs stone (47) has billowing breeches, based on an oriental cut, no doubt worn with gartered stockings. Linen pants and shirts are mentioned in the medieval sagas. Over these was worn a tunic reaching anywhere from mid-thigh to below the knee. A belt completed the basic outfit, and from it hung such objects as a knife, comb or purse. The dress of poorer people such as slaves was, however, much simpler – perhaps no more than a blanket-like garment, with a hole for the head and tied about with a cord.

Leather shoes and ankle-boots for both men and women are known from several finds; they were secured by a lace round the top or by a small toggle. Whether found at Oseberg, Lund, Hedeby or York, there is little variety in the simple, but functional types. Hats of various forms were also worn, but less is known about these, although some of the helmets worn by men shown in the pictures may be little more than leather caps. Some men wore their hair to neck-length, holding it back with an ornamental head-band. But others must have preferred a shorter style, with a fringe and a 'bared neck', for men in eleventh-century England were being criticised for adopting this 'Danish' cut. Beards and moustaches were carefully tended (64). Married women were expected to keep their heads covered, but some pictures suggest that their hair was still worn long, gathered up in a knot at the back of the head (43).

A man would have given as much thought – or more – to his weapons as to his clothes. He is unlikely to have often been without them, for as the poem *Hávamál* says: 'A man should never move an inch from his weapons when out in the fields, for he never knows when he will need his spear'. It was the spear, and not the traditional axe, that was the commonest of all Viking weapons. Spears were used for hunting as well as fighting and come in all grades, from plain iron points to masterpieces of the weapon-smith's craft, with lavishly ornamented sockets (63). Light spears were made for throwing and the heavier ones were for thrusting. Some have wing-like projections from their sockets, a type derived from the Carolingian Empire. Perhaps it is these that are referred to in a Greenlandic verse of the eleventh century, or later:

> Full they were of fighters
> and flashing bucklers,
> western war-lances
> and wound-blades Frankish.

60 FAR LEFT *Richly ornamented brooch for a man's cloak.*

61 LEFT *A ringed pin from Birka imitates western fashions.*

The 'wound-blades Frankish' were high-quality sword-blades imported from the Rhineland and used for some of the finest Viking swords. For the sword was the most important of all weapons. Great care and expense might be lavished on the decoration of its hilt. The guards could be encrusted with precious metals (62, 83), or carved out of antler or ivory (98). But even the plainest iron sword (63) was a supremely functional object of devastating efficiency. It was designed as a single-

handed slashing weapon and had a blade about three feet long. To be ready for use, a sword was carried in a scabbard often finely ornamented with metal mounts, slung from a belt or a baldric across the shoulder.

The next most important offensive weapon was the axe – a weapon much associated with the Vikings and portrayed in the hands of some of the raiders on the Lindisfarne stone (2). Various forms were used, some adapted from the woodman's axe (which itself would be a useful weapon in an emergency), but others specially designed. The broad-axe, like that from the River Thames at London (63), was a fearsome weapon of immense force when wielded with strong arms.

Bows and arrows were used for fighting as well as for hunting; a massive longbow recently excavated at Hedeby would have been a weapon of considerable power. Some arrowheads were designed for maximum armour-piercing force and one such may account for a hole in the iron helmet from Gjermundbu. This Norwegian find is the only complete Viking helmet known to survive. In shape it is little more than a rounded cap with a nose- and eye-guard, like monstrous spectacles. No horns, and no wings, such as are frequently and mistakenly provided by all too romantic modern imaginations! The truth of this is confirmed by the many contemporary pictures of helmets, from those on the Gotlandic stones (8, 47) to those of the Middleton and Sigtuna warriors (30, 64).

The chief protection for the body was provided by the shield. These were circular wooden boards, often painted, with a central iron boss to protect the hand-grip. Mail-shirts are known (there was one in the Gjermundbu grave), but were probably worn only by the rich.

The Viking warrior commemorated by a tenth-century cross at Middleton in Yorkshire (30) displays many of these elements of dress and equipment, although he is crudely carved. He wears breeches or tight trousers, with a belt from which hangs a large knife that would have had a leather sheath similar to one found recently in York (65); on his head is a conical helmet. To his left are arrayed his shield, sword and axe, with his spear on his other side.

Fighting was a hand-to-hand affair and Viking tactics have been described as 'consisting largely of bashing hell out of the opposing side'. There was little unnecessary heroism; it was best to make a quick getaway on occasion so as to live to fight another day. The use of horsemen in battle increased during the Viking Age and there are a number of rich burials which contain one or two horses and the necessary equipment, known from tenth-century Denmark and from Birka. As much care was taken with the decoration of the riding-equipment of such men as was given to their weapons. Matched pairs of stirrups and of spurs (66) are found in graves. Adam of Bremen had heard in the eleventh century that the Swedes were 'very great warriors both on horses and on ships'. There can be no doubt that the qualities of their ships and their weapons were an important factor in the successes of the Vikings on their raids and military expeditions.

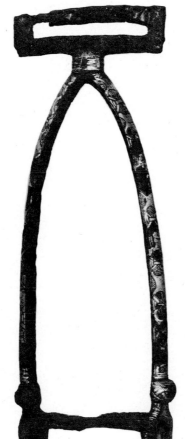

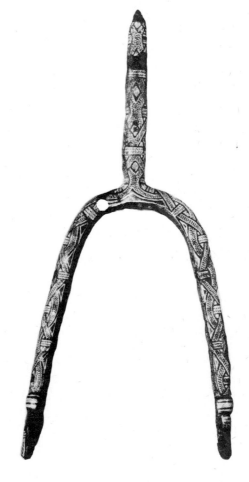

64 LEFT *The helmeted head of a warrior, found at Sigtuna, Sweden.*

65 ABOVE *Leather sheath from York with Anglo-Scandinavian ornament.*

66 RIGHT *Silver-encrusted riding equipment from Denmark.*

8 Kings and Coinage

The Viking Age resounds with the names of great leaders, and kings bearing exotic-sounding nicknames. Some receive cryptic mention in contemporary chronicles. Some appear larger than life in medieval Icelandic sagas, composed long after the Viking Age was over. As adventurers, exiles, leaders of raids or rulers of kingdoms they sometimes move about the Viking world with startling speed. In modern terms many died very young, and often by violence. Rarely were they safe from their enemies or followers.

Until the late Viking period we know little definite about territorial organisation and political control within Scandinavia itself. A few facts relating to the earlier period are gleaned from accounts written by visiting monks or merchants. Where the Vikings were active abroad some account of their organisation survives, but some of the terminology employed may not always be clear to us. The area about which most is known, Iceland, was a republic from its formal establishment in 930 until 1262, and was effectively run by a few powerful families and their supporters, manipulating the assemblies of freemen.

We may recognise early leaders from the intrinsic value and symbolic prestige of what was buried in their graves. At Valsgärde in Uppland is a sequence of burials of armed men, often with richly worked ornaments, harness and a range of equipment, each buried in a boat. Here from the seventh century a powerful family maintained its outstanding position, but we do not know what role its members played, nor how they were designated. There appears to have been a series of regional chiefs in parts of Scandinavia, whatever their titles and relative position, well into the Viking Age. At other Scandinavian sites a rich burial may be isolated, implying perhaps that power acquired by one individual was not handed on locally and died with him. Some leaders were buried abroad where they were killed or suddenly died. At the mouth of the Loire, on the Ile de Groix, a ship was burned with numerous shields and weapons, the tools of a smith, silver and gold fragments and gold-embroidered cloth. Perhaps the cremation burial was that of the leader of a group of sea-raiders. He may have achieved this position by status inherited at home or by prestige acquired abroad.

The chronicles often refer to kings, chiefs, or leaders of an army, but what the limits were on their power we do not know. Although in general terms the stratification of society and differences in wealth are reflected in the contents of graves, it is not possible to equate the rich grave accessories directly with status. When the Scandinavian states were being established under a central king, traditional territorial magnates, such as the earls who

67 *Silver pennies of the Viking kingdom of York.*

a) ABOVE LEFT *Obverse of a penny with the name of St Peter, showing a sword and Thor's hammer* (c. *910*).

b) ABOVE RIGHT *Obverse of a penny of Raienalt, showing a bearded effigy* (c. *920*).

c) CENTRE LEFT *Reverse of a penny of Raienalt, showing a bow and arrow* (c. *920*).

d) CENTRE RIGHT *Obverse of a penny of Anlaf Guthfrithsson with royal title* CUNUNC, *showing a raven* (c. *940*).

e) BELOW LEFT *Reverse of a penny of Anlaf Sihtricsson, showing a standard with a cross* (c. *942*).

f) BELOW RIGHT *Obverse of a penny of Anlaf Sihtricsson, showing a triquetra ornament* (c. *942*).

were nominally subordinate, or army leaders, were as rich and almost as independent as the royal authority. Hence the importance to the royal power of sole control of towns and taxing trade, or of amassing wealth by more systematic raiding than their subordinates.

In the Viking period power depended on prestige and the support of other, less powerful men. In a descending hierarchy of relationships it extended to the level of the free, weapon-bearing farmer – even kings could not ignore the feelings of the assemblies of freemen. Followers were obtained by successfully acquiring wealth which could be redistributed to the benefit of supporters. Returning home after seasonal hit-and-run raids or after longer periods in exile, men with silver and prestige were able to break into the inherited social order based on wealth in land. As the scale of warfare became larger and more complex, raiding parties grew to armies which wintered away from home.

Organisation was needed to ensure supplies and make tactical decisions. When armies settled territory, or permanently occupied towns, they were vulnerable to counter-attack and required territorial organisation for defence. To protect trade-routes and centres which they were then taxing rather than raiding, Viking leaders had to organise against still predatory Scandinavians. Some leaders and petty kings lived in their towns – from Dublin to Kiev – as 'city states', while others were controlled by royal representatives such as Heirgar, who erected the first church at Birka. At Hedeby has been found an outstanding grave of the tenth century, with weapons (83) and a glass drinking-vessel, placed in a chamber under a ship. Whether this is of a local ruler, or of the Danish king's representative in the town, is unknown.

We hear of dominant families, men linked by blood ties or marriage, who raised large armies and whose ambitions were for territorial aggrandisement. Attempts by its kings to dominate not only Norway but also Norse settlements, by delegating earls to rule provinces or by sending out their sons, are typical of Norway. These politics were complicated by claims based on inheritance and by alliances contrary to family obligations. In the late Viking period Scandinavia itself became the scene of fierce conflicts between rivals for kingdoms and between kings. For it was the personal power of the man, and the support he might enjoy, however temporarily, that held a kingdom.

Coins can be used to supplement the sparse written records in the study of this formative period of political history. From their inscriptions it is possible to identify coins minted under rulers known from documents, and thus also record figures whose historical identity is otherwise lost to us. Many coins are struck with the name of their moneyer and the place of minting, and the dates of striking many of them can now be established with relative precision. From analysing the dates of their burial in hoards we can identify episodes of insecurity when people hid their wealth, and could not return to claim it.

The earliest Scandinavian coinage was probably minted at Hedeby about the year 825 (68a). Its coins were struck between two iron dies on thin silver blanks. Their designs copied and modified elements from the

68a *Coin (reused as pendant), struck at Hedeby, c. 825.*

68b *Penny of Guthrum after he was baptised Athelstan, struck c. 888–90.*

68c & d *Obverses of a penny and halfpenny of Cnut, struck at York, c. 900.*

68e *Penny with the name of St Martin, struck at Lincoln, c. 915.*

68f *Penny of Sihtric III, struck at Dublin, c. 997.*

coins of the Carolingian Empire with which the town had strong trade-links. Rarely found outside early trading-sites, they appear to have been a short-lived issue. The first Viking coins in England were struck in those Danish areas where there were strong commercial contacts with the Anglo-Saxons who had a highly developed silver coinage. Dating from the late 880s, after the partition of England, coins were struck in the southern Danelaw by King Guthrum (68b). They bear his baptismal name, Athelstan, which had been bestowed on him by the English King Alfred after he defeated the Vikings in 878. Like many subsequent Viking issues, they imitated contemporary Anglo-Saxon coins.

At Quentovic, a flourishing trading port on the Channel coast of France, an imitative coinage was established by the Viking occupants copying local Carolingian issues. The designs of the earliest coins from York, struck just before 900, were also mainly Carolingian in inspiration, suggesting a North Sea trading interest. But as relations with Anglo-Saxon England grew stronger it was the designs of the Anglo-Saxon coins which were more often imitated. As in the Anglo-Saxon coinage there were two denominations: the silver penny and halfpenny (68c, d).

From 919 until 954 York was ruled periodically by Irish-Norse elements from Dublin and by Norwegian and Anglo-Saxon kings. The forging of an axis from Dublin and the Irish Sea across Lancashire, over the Pennines to York and so the North Sea, became politically and militarily significant in Norwegian plans for domination. Coins were issued in the names of all three groups. That management of the coinage was essentially a commercial non-political matter is shown by the consecutive employment of some of the same moneyers despite these changes in political control. In the circumstances of the tenth century a reliable coinage was essential for the cosmopolitan trade-centre that York became. In the area of the Five Boroughs the earliest Viking issues, although they are blundered copies of Anglo-Saxon coins, are struck to a lighter weight standard. At Lincoln rare coins bear the mint signature of the town and a representation of the sword of a locally revered saint (68e). Later, Derby issued coins for both Viking and Anglo-Saxon kings. Curiously very few of these Viking coins are found in Scandinavia, being used mainly in Irish Sea and Anglo-Saxon trade. This phase of Viking coinage was brought to an end when in 954 Eirík 'Bloodaxe', the last Viking King of York, was finally expelled, and the town incorporated into the English kingdom. There were no further independent Viking coinages in England.

After 973, regular type-changes were an aspect of Anglo-Saxon coinage administration. Changes of design were copied, one after the other, by the Viking coinage of silver pennies that was started in Dublin in about 997 under Sihtric III 'Silkbeard' (68f). After 980 when the Battle of Tara broke Dublin's political power, trade had increased in importance. The purpose of the coinage was to facilitate trade around the Irish Sea, especially with the Anglo-Saxon areas, whose coins had previously been used in large numbers. The early Dublin coins copied the current Anglo-Saxon type and when it was periodically changed Dublin followed suit to make its own coins more widely acceptable. The waning commercial fortunes of Dublin are reflected in growing lightness of weight, and the degeneration of legends into illiteracy, as shown by an otherwise splendid example of about 1065 (68g).

It is a disappointment that the faces – mostly in profile – which dominate Viking coins are merely copied from Anglo-Saxon coins. Often the head remains the same time after time while the name of the ruler changes. One possible concession to realism may be the head of Raienalt, ruler of York, on coins struck about the year 915 (67b).

The artistic quality of some coins, as well as their purely technical excellence, is remarkable. We know from their names that some moneyers of Viking coins were of Frankish or Anglo-Saxon origin; and the inscriptions on the coins were usually in Latin – the king would be called '*Rex*' and only rarely by his old Norse title '*Cununc*'. Inscriptions in runic characters such as on a mid eleventh-century Danish coin of Sven Estridsson are rare (68h). Designs on the reverse side were sometimes copied, more or less closely, from Carolingian coins, for instance the monogram of the name 'Carolus' (68j). Although some Viking coins faithfully copy the current Anglo-Saxon types, others have highly original designs. Sometimes issues show a standard, triquetra, bow and arrow, sword or Thor's hammer, as in some of the York coins, while the raven occurs on others (67d). But in general, Christian iconography such as the simple equal-armed cross or more specifically the Lamb of God, would proclaim the adherence to Christianity of the Scandinavian rulers. Some of the earliest Viking issues in East Anglia struck in the 890s commemorate the martyred Anglo-Saxon King Edmund, sanctified after his execution in 870 by Vikings (68k).

The prestige and propaganda value of coins should not be under-estimated. It is no accident that Scandinavian coins continued to copy Anglo-Saxon issues after the emergence of the early national kingdoms about AD 1000, nor that Byzantine influences can be seen in Scandinavian coins most strongly from about 1050.

We first read of Viking kings in the area of the later kingdom of Denmark, but it is not clear how great an area they controlled. By the early ninth century, King Godfred was active along the strategic sea trade-routes, attacking Frisia and the West Slavs. In 808 he destroyed the town of Reric in Slav territory, and planted the merchants in his own settlement at Hedeby. He may have begun, or strengthened, an already existing timber and earth rampart defending the southern frontier. Known as the 'Danevirke', this defensive system became a complex series of earthworks (fig. 7). In south-east Jutland a great land route, the Hærvej, leading directly northwards through Jutland enters the kingdom of Denmark. Here the Danevirke defended it, blocking a gap between the Schlei Estuary and the rivers protecting the south-western part of the Jutland Peninsula. Relations with the expanding Empire to the south and west were always tense and Jutland was occasionally invaded by land from this quarter. Harald Klak, exiled from Denmark, was converted, and on his return in 826 brought the monk Ansgar with a mission. Political pressure

68g *Penny with blundered legends, struck at Dublin,* c. 1065.

68h *Penny of Sven Estridsson, struck at Lund,* c. 1065–74.

68j *Reverse of a penny with Carolus monogram, struck at York,* c. 900.

68k *Penny commemorating St Edmund, struck in East Anglia,* c. 890.

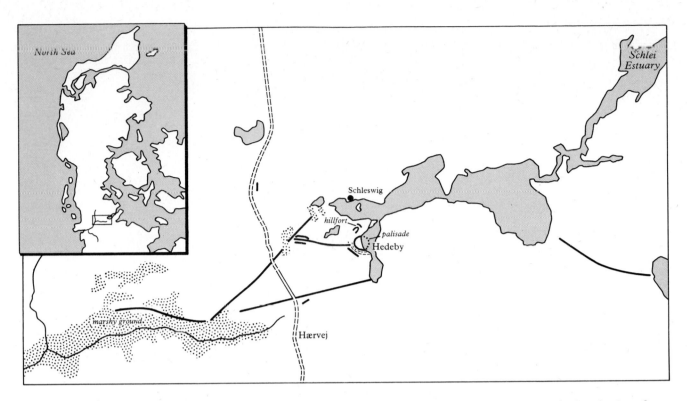

Fig. 7 The earthwork defences of the southern border of the kingdom of Denmark.

on Horik I was probably behind his granting royal permission in 850 for a church to be erected at Hedeby.

It was the proud boast of Harald 'Bluetooth' (*c*. 950–985?) that he 'won the whole of Denmark and Norway for himself and made the Danes Christians'. This brief summary of his own achievements he set in runes on a massive granite boulder in the shape of a three-sided pyramid eight feet high, at the royal burial-place at Jelling in east-central Jutland. He was probably responsible for removing the bones of his mother and father, Gorm and Thyra, from their pagan burial-mound, and placing them within a newly built wooden church. This was sited within a massive group of stones, shaped like a ship, that linked two immense flat-topped mounds on the site (69). From another runestone we know that he was once married to Tova, daughter of a strategically placed Slav king. Certainly Harald was successful diplomatically but the land frontier was vulnerable to attack and the Danevirke was extended.

Hedeby, which formed a tempting prize and had been occupied early in the tenth century by a Swedish king, was from the later tenth century protected by a large semicircular earthwork enclosing an area of about sixty acres and by further earthworks on its southern side. These ditches and banks, sometimes faced with timber, with timber superstructure and gateways, are evidence of great power. Not only resources in manpower and technical skills were involved, but a degree of planning that could only be controlled by a king. Within Hedeby the regular layout suggests strong control at a local level. The town was the terminal of sea-routes and protected by a large wooden palisade encircling the harbour. Around Danish coasts there are local defences such as massed palisades, some of

which may be of Viking date, while the barrier of wrecks deliberately sunk near Skuldelev to block the fjord approach to Roskilde dates to the eleventh century. A group of four circular earthworks, situated strategically by important routes and often naturally protected, were probably part of a further system. These sites protected groups of large, regularly planned timber buildings which have in the past been interpreted as barracks while troops were assembled for the invasion, of England in the early eleventh century. But all four sites had a short occupation during the last quarter of the tenth century, women have been found buried in their cemeteries, and there is a scarcity of weapons. This is not the kind of evidence expected from a military site. Research shows that at Fyrkat (70) the internal structures were used as stores, iron-smithies and fine-metal workshops, as well as for housing people. It may have been an administrative and tax-gathering centre, supplying the king's men, and this may have been the function of the other similar sites (fig. 8).

From about the same period a great wooden bridge, over half a mile long, was built across a boggy valley at Ravning Enge in eastern Jutland to

69 *The tenth-century Danish royal burial site at Jelling.*

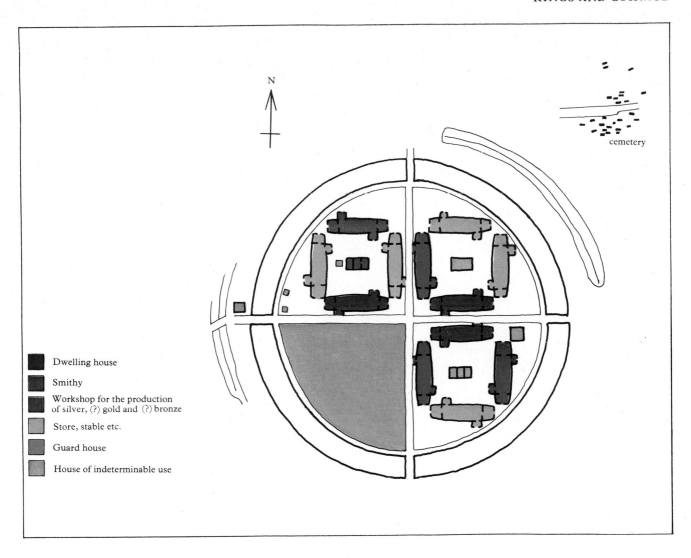

cemetery

Dwelling house

Smithy

Workshop for the production
of silver, (?) gold and (?) bronze

Store, stable etc.

Guard house

House of indeterminable use

Fig. 8 *The function of
buildings within the late
tenth-century ring-fort at
Fyrkat, Denmark,
interpreted from excavation.*

70 OVERLEAF *A view of the
reconstructed rampart.*

improve north–south land communications. While the dating of some of
the sites and earthworks is not precise enough to attribute them to Harald
rather than his son, it is likely that Harald's organisation allowed rapid
further growth in Denmark. His son, Svein 'Forkbeard' (*c.* 985–1014),
mounted massive raids on England from the 980s. The Danegeld was
systematically extorted – masses of silver in blackmail payment – largely in
coin. It flooded into Denmark (including southern Sweden) and seems to
have stimulated the first regal coinage in the kingdom. After the massacre
of Danes on St Brice's Day 1002 by the English, among whose victims was
Svein's sister, he determined to conquer the country and in 1014 he was
accepted as King of England. Only weeks later he died.

With Knut Sveinsson 'the Great' (1014–1035) there was a personal
union of England, Norway and Denmark. Nominally the area he
controlled stretched from the North Cape of Arctic Norway to south-west
England to south-east Sweden. The extent and nature of control over his
kingdom may be seen from the coinage: a regular network of mints to serve
local needs was established in Denmark on the Anglo-Saxon model, and

Anglo-Saxon moneyers are recorded on coins struck at Lund (681). In England dies were often made at regional centres, types were standardised from one end of the kingdom to the other, and changes in type took place uniformly. The organisation this implies is extremely efficient, the Anglo-Scandinavian kingdom being in no way less developed than any other in northern Europe. Knut was a European king and was accepted as their equal, visiting Rome for the coronation of the German emperor, Conrad, in 1027. He formed dynastic marriages, but the unity disintegrated with his death in 1035. From 1042 to 1046 King Magnus of Norway ruled Denmark and defeated a Slav invasion in 1043, but then there was war between the Norwegians and the Danes under Sven Estridsson. Hedeby was sacked in 1050 and Århus several times, until in 1064 a treaty acknowledged the separation of both states. In 1066 Hedeby was sacked by the Slavs and never recovered, its position being taken over by near-by Schleswig.

681 *Penny of Knut 'the Great', struck at Lund, c. 1018–20.*

In England Anglo-Saxon kings ruled from 1042 until 1066. Scandinavian mercenary troops were paid off by Edward 'the Confessor' in 1051, ending the flow of English silver payments which went to Denmark. This event was marked by an immediate increase in the weight of the English penny being produced at the time. In 1066 a Norwegian attack was routed by the English, but a Norman army under their Duke William succeeded in conquering the kingdom. Sven Estridsson attacked England in 1069–70, but made peace after William had ruthlessly ravaged areas with Scandinavian population. England was drawn into European French politics by the Normans, but for two decades there were abortive raids and threats of invasion from Scandinavia. In 1085 Knut II, 'the Holy', of Denmark failed in his attempt to win over the strong Scandinavian population of northern and eastern England, and the threat of Scandinavian interference never seriously revived.

In Norway a ninth-century centre of power is represented along the Oslo Fjord by a small number of outstanding ship-burials under large mounds. One young woman, buried with an aged woman servant at Oseberg, may even have been Queen Åsa, the grandmother of Harald 'Finehair'. The attempts by Harald 'Finehair' in the later ninth century to impose central control by force ultimately failed with his death. In Norway native coinage is first associated with Olaf Tryggvason in the last years of the tenth century. He led a turbulent life, which gave rise to many stories about him, including tales of outlawry and fighting among the Slavs, the English and the Norwegians; in the end, he was drowned in the Baltic. He was the first Norwegian to be involved in taking the Danegeld from England and, as is the case in Denmark, this stimulus seems to have started a native coinage. He had attempted to enforce Christianity upon the Norwegians, and Olaf Haraldsson (1015–30; known as St Olaf soon after his death) was killed while trying to impose his political rule and Christian beliefs over Norway. Magnus 'the Good' made Norway independent of Denmark from 1035, but it was on the initiative of Harald 'the Ruthless' (1047–66) that a strong local coinage was introduced (68m). But much of this coinage was very base silver as analysis has shown, and a saga story tells of the reluctance of one Halldór Snorrason to accept it: 'Why should I

68m *Penny of Harald 'the Ruthless', struck c. 1047–55.*

serve him [Harald] any longer when I don't even get my pay unadulterated?,' to which the reply is: 'You did not behave decently when you threw the money down on the straw . . . the King regards this as an insult.' But after a while he was paid in fine weighed silver. Harald died at the Battle of Stamford Bridge trying to gain the kingdom of England in 1066.

For Sweden there is very little information about the early Viking period. Accounts of Ansgar's mission to Scandinavia in the second quarter of the ninth century name King Bjørn who controlled the town of Birka. Like Hedeby, the town was imposed on an existing site, and was successor to a previous trading and craft centre near by. In the tenth century it was fortified with an earthwork surrounding about thirty acres and appears to have had some harbour defences. Olaf Sköttkonung (994–1022), who was converted in 1008 to Christianity, instituted a native coinage but it did not endure. Gotland, which was independent and without a ruler or central urban site, continued to import masses of English and German coins but did not mint independently.

The dates chosen to mark the close of the Viking Age vary from area to area, but in Scandinavia it is often set about 1050. The eleventh century is a period when royal intervention in encouraging growth in towns in Scandinavia increased. Birka had been replaced by Sigtuna, Hedeby by Schleswig, and little remained on the old sites. New towns were established which nearly all survived into the modern period as important centres: in Norway – Trondheim, Bergen and Oslo; in Sweden – Sigtuna, Lund and Skara; in Denmark – Ålborg, Odense and Roskilde among others. They sometimes became the seat of a bishop as well as a mint. In inscriptions of the late Viking Age, we read of craft or merchant guilds – organised groups of men in towns bound by common interests. The emergence of national states with centralised political structures required administrative centres, a standardised coinage and regulated trade. The transition to such medieval forms of institution had beginnings in the Viking Age. Christianity was rapidly adopted and promulgated by the later kings because of the mutual support each hierarchical organisation offered. External intervention also played a part, and the aggressive policy of conversion by the Church was mirrored in German territorial expansion which was always a threat to the Kingdom of Denmark.

9 Viking Crafts

One of the characteristics of the Viking Age is the increasingly intensive use of local resources, which included raw materials for craft production as well as agricultural products. Primary raw materials and semi-finished items were supplied to a growing number of urban workshops. The products of these craftsmen have long been known and recent excavations in towns have revealed the workshops where many of these pieces must have been made. Basic raw materials were worked as well as more exotic ones, and a variety of service activities developed in the towns. For with the growth of long-distance trade in luxury items, centred on urban sites, there came a demand for various semi-specialist craft industries. Trading in the products of these workshops, and marketing a range of non-agricultural products, an intense local trade between Scandinavian settlements grew up.

As the period progressed the network of trading-links grew more complex and the numbers of communities involved increased. Agricultural settlements, which contained the bulk of Viking population, were largely self-sufficient in foodstuffs, clothing and building materials but not all were able to supply their requirements in iron, or salt which was used in preserving meat and fish. Communities gaining their living by trading and craft specialisation needed an outside surplus of agricultural produce to support them. The circulation of luxury and urban manufactured goods was a stimulus to producing readily exchangeable items. The range of urban crafts, their quality and volume of production was quite distinct from those of the countryside.

The availability of slave or unfree labour on farming estates sometimes released the owner from essential farm work, allowing him to engage in other activities to supplement his income. In areas where the land was agriculturally marginal and unproductive, this would ensure extra security in providing essential supplies. The Norwegian, Ottar, is an example of a farmer who also engaged in seasonal hunting and trading (p. 41. Hunting for fur to supply the luxury trade explains the expansion of settlement into the forests and uplands of Scandinavia. Graves here contain hunting equipment including specialised arrows with blunt ends to prevent damage to fur, and broad blades to cut tendons.

A further stimulus to settlement in the mountain areas of Norway and the agriculturally barren areas of central and northern Sweden was the presence there of surface bog-iron, which was not found in agriculturally rich limestone soils. Ores were deposited in the peat-bogs by centuries of percolating ground-water with iron salts in solution. Because of the presence of forest timber the ores could be reduced with charcoal on the

71 *A group of tools deposited in the grave of a tenth-century Norwegian weapon-smith.*

spot to produce a spongy iron slag, which was then further refined. Heaps of waste slag and burnt clay from the structures of furnaces mark these primitive working areas. Iron ore was mined in Sweden during the late Viking period but both the technology and exact date at which it commenced is obscure. Copper ores may also have been mined.

Many farm estates provided their own iron from local bog deposits, but iron had been traded since the fifth and sixth centuries to early centres such as Helgö from more peripheral settlement areas. To supply the demand for high-grade iron in large quantities, the sources of production had to be expanded even before the Viking period. There was a growing need for agricultural tools so that more food could be produced for an expanding population, and, for example, for woodsmen's axes used in clearing the forests. Specialised hunting equipment, riding-gear and weapons for the prosperous farmers were widely in demand, and a whole range of elaborate domestic items in iron began to appear, such as, for example, the lamp from Hennum and the spit from Lund (72). The rich graves in iron-extracting areas show that local smithing technology had reached a high level of skill. An iron cauldron on a chain from Bengtsarvet in the iron-rich Swedish province of Dalarna is an outstanding example (35). Iron blanks in the rough shape of hoes, chisels or axes were produced, perhaps representing a value or weight equivalent in various areas of Norway and Sweden, and widely traded. A group of twelve axe-shaped blanks on a spruce-wood carrying-stave found in eastern Jutland had been imported from northern Scandinavia. Sites such as Hedeby have masses of slag from iron-smithing, concentrated especially on the edges of the densely packed settlement to avoid the risk of fire during working. The massive iron anchor from the trading site of Ribe is a *tour de force* of the smith's craft.

The increased production of iron coincided with a greater specialisation of iron tools used by various craftsmen. A range of basic forms was successfully established and in consequence varied little until the Industrial Revolution. Much of the everyday wood- and iron-working on the farm appears to have been done locally, but itinerant craftsmen, competent to undertake a variety of specialist jobs and hawking some items, travelled around the countryside. A wooden chest from Mästermyr on Gotland contained the tools of one such man, lost perhaps while crossing a frozen bog during the winter. The objects found imply a wide variety of skills: heavy iron-smithing; light work involving nail-making; the repair of bronze cauldrons (shears to cut the sheet patches were included). He could also perform various woodworking tasks, including joinery and carpentry, using the axes, adzes, light saws and plane, and possibly also made barrels.

Legends and archaeology indicate the importance of the smith in the community, particularly the specialist in weapon-making. From Bygland in Norway, a tenth-century grave shows the wealth and status that a skilled craftsman who specialised in metalworking could acquire. The grave contained four swords, four spears, shield-bosses, axes, arrows and knives, and a range of riding-gear. Presumably these were part of the smith's stock. The tools (71) suggest both heavy and light iron-smithing, and included specialist equipment for making axes. Recent research into the technology and composition of iron objects has revealed great sophistication and skill in craftsmanship. The making of weapons, especially swords, was a highly skilled task. The finest, sometimes marked with the maker's name, were imported from the Rhineland, where skill had developed over centuries. The best Scandinavian and imported blades were pattern-welded, that is formed of numbers of individual iron strips twisted and welded together to form a composite whole. There was a long process of building up the blade from welding together in a particular sequence strips of metal in groups of different qualities. The finished surface when polished showed a variegated pattern from the succession of welds – this proved the quality of the workmanship and hence reliability in battle. The process of complex hammering removed impurities which would have weakened the metal, causing it to break with impact; and its structure gave it great flexibility. The addition of carbon to the iron in the furnace produced hard steel, which was used on the outer edges to form a sharp cutting-blade.

A versatile soft and easily worked material which increased in importance during the Viking period was soapstone, or steatite. This soft, easily carved rock outcrops especially in south-west Norway and might have been worked seasonally. Even large vessels were blocked-out in the living rock and trimmed roughly to shape on the spot. Some of them were transported in this state to Kaupang, where fragments show that they were finished off there before being exported or redistributed in the countryside. Vessels from Hedeby and Birka show that they were in use in these trading-centres. One of the simplest forms was the hemispherical bowl, often very finely finished with a rifling technique on the interior (73).

72 RIGHT *Iron spit for roasting meat, from Lund.*

73 FAR RIGHT *Soapstone bowl with rifled interior, incised on the rim with maker's mark, from Landvikvannet, Norway.*

Makers' or owners' marks on the rim show their value. Other more complex forms included handled vessels or rectangular forms which demonstrate the expertise of the carver.

The ability to carve soapstone into complex shapes resulted in a range of artefacts often decorated on their surfaces, the furnace-stone from Snaptun, for example (46). The delicate shaping of a tear-shaped line-weight from Hedeby shows how aesthetically perfect a simple, functional object could become. A further source of soapstone which was worked intensively is in the Shetland Islands; on the site of Jarlshof a range of simple vessels and artefacts such as spindle-whorls and miniature lamps has been found. Objects of soapstone found at York may have been imported from either source. A further source was in Greenland, and a soapstone weight incised with a Thor's hammer from Brattahlíd is amongst evidence of its being worked in this remote area.

Other types of stone were used for making specialised artefacts, such as delicately fashioned pendants from Birka; they were carefully selected for their beautiful colouring. Some may have been amulets, while others served as pin- or needle-sharpeners. The black stones could be used as touchstones to test the colour and hence purity of gold. Larger whetstones for sharpening iron tools were an important part of everyday equipment and were widely traded, especially as varying degrees of quality in sharpening were required to produce a finely honed edge from a newly forged blade. Examples from Norway have been identified at York. A Viking shipwreck near Kaupang had a group of whetstones among its cargo. Whether there was a bulk trade in such items or whether they represent sporadic individual initiative is not certain, but at Hedeby there is a considerable quantity of Norwegian schist.

Raw materials such as carnelian and crystal may have been imported to places like Hedeby for working into beads, as well as being brought in as finished items. Local amber was worked for costume jewellery, ornaments and special possessions, for example, gaming-pieces. Ranging in colour from a dark, reddish brown to a translucent straw, the colouring and tactile properties of amber made it a treasured material long before the Viking period. Amber is the fossilised resin from ancient pine forests, long submerged under the sea. The material could be gathered irregularly along the North Sea coasts of East Anglia, south-west Jutland and the shores of the south Baltic, having been washed loose from its deposits by sea currents, especially during violent storms. It was worked in specialist workshops at Ribe, York, Hedeby and Birka, especially into small delicate items (74). Workshop debris shows that it was cut, carved and turned with many of the techniques used in working jet and bone. Shapes such as the axe pendant from Hedeby (74) and the cat from Birka may be charms. A small group of amber statuettes and animal representations in the round show how expertly the craftsmen made the most of its particular properties.

The ivory tusk of the walrus was also a prized material, and well suited to three-dimensional carving. The seated figure from Lund, which may be of the god Freyr and is possibly a gaming-piece, is a delicate example of the

74 ABOVE RIGHT *Amber: unfinished and finished items, worked at Hedeby.*

75 BELOW RIGHT *Walrus-ivory figure from Lund.*

possibilities presented by its surface texture and quality (75). It was much in demand in western Europe, and was a valuable export from the northern Scandinavian settlements, especially Greenland.

In complete contrast is the black lustrous surface of jet. This is another fossilised deposit, closely related to shale. It is exposed in cliffs near Whitby in eastern Yorkshire, and some was worked at York during the Viking period. This appears to have been the only source, so that finds from Scotland and Norway are evidence of internal trading. The lightly incised gaming-piece from Bawdsey in East Anglia is one of the larger worked pieces, while armlets from Castletown in Scotland and Høyland in Norway show the versatility of the medium. Pendants in the form of a coiled snake (16) and lathe-turned beads occur. One outstanding piece of three-dimensional carving in jet comes from Tresfjorden in Norway (16). The treatment of the two bears gambolling is naturalistic, and may be considered along with other unusual representations, like the amber cat and elk-antler bird from Birka.

A completely different technique is the use of glass for small trinkets and ornaments. Most glass vessels were imported. Broken fragments of such vessels may have been used as raw material in Scandinavian glass-working. At Paviken on Gotland and at Birka glass mosaic cubes have been found which were imported, perhaps from as far away as northern Italy. Originally used for mosaic floor and wall coverings, they were now melted down and reused. Glass was worked at Hedeby, but the details of this are obscure. Excavations at Ribe have uncovered a local workshop which produced multi-coloured glass beads. The mosaic effect of this kind of glass was achieved by a series of minutely complex actions. Each different pattern was the result of fusing composite coloured glass rods in varying combinations, and these rods themselves were formed by bunching and folding over others, then drawing out the hot glass into the form of a narrow rod. A necklace such as that from Eidem (76) can be seen as the product of great expertise and skill, as well as being an intrinsically beautiful piece of costume jewellery. Simpler glass beads and glass paste were also made on Viking urban sites. Other trinkets of glass such as finger-rings were made by Anglo-Scandinavian craftsmen in Lincoln and elsewhere.

Clay was used to make a range of everyday items. Baked clay weights for the weaving-loom, and small spindle-whorls used in making thread are common on Viking sites. Crucibles for melting metals, and crude discs to guard the bellow's nozzle from the heat of the furnace were specialised uses of clay in metalworking. But a developed mass-production industry for pottery was lacking over much of Scandinavia until the very end of the Viking period and when it did appear, in Lund for instance, it was under strong Slav influence (34). Imported pottery vessels were costly and not in general use, being largely restricted to towns and other trading-centres.

Soapstone, bronze and iron fulfilled some specialised functions, but leather and wood must have been the principal everyday materials. Lathe-turned vessels such as the mug and platter from York are representatives of one form of specialised manufacture. The stave-built tub from Lund with

76 *A necklace of richly coloured glass beads from Eidem, Norway.*

its elaborate construction-marks and binding is another. Ladles and scoops, often with decorated handle terminals, and made to fine proportions, are found. Delicately worked spoons are at the smaller end of the size range.

It is quite clear that the wood used for these different vessels – oak, maple, ash and others – was carefully chosen to suit techniques of production and use. The range of artefacts preserved in the ship-burial at Oseberg in Norway, and above all the high quality of the applied art carved on many of them, shows the variety of manufactured goods available to the well-off. Urban excavation shows how highly developed woodworking came to be among the crafts practised. The number of different tools from Mästermyr (p. 132) suggests great expertise, and the fragment of carved plank, perhaps part of a piece of furniture, from Trondheim shows how wood-carving lent itself to artistic expression. Since organic material is so rarely preserved, the panels from Flatatunga (114) and the magnificently carved doorway from the church at Urnes (115) are representatives of a whole range of lost material. The use of timber in fortification, shipbuilding and house construction was on a larger scale, requiring different skills. The supply of timber in these quantities implies a developed logistic and transport system to meet requirements (p. 123).

Another aspect of large-scale working is stone-carving. Although painted memorial-stones appear on Gotland, the use of slabs of stone as a medium for Viking carved decoration, especially for memorial-stones, is the result of Anglo-Saxon and Celtic influence. Stone-carving reached a peak in northern England and the Isle of Man. Not only was it worked in urban contexts as at York (77), but rural schools developed for local patrons. At York slabs of stone left from the Roman period were reused, and it is likely that fresh blocks were hewn and transported from near-by quarries. On the Isle of Man soft slabs of slate were treated in a manner akin to carving wooden planks.

The intensive working of bone, antler and horn into a whole series of artefacts which were functional as well as decorative shows how the Viking utilised all available natural resources. Cattle or horse bones, flattened on the lower surface and perforated for attachment to the feet, were used as skates (27). They are particularly common in Lund and are found in graves at Birka. Skeletal bone was not a popular medium for delicate reworking and was often used for crude tools such as pointed awls, or sleeve handles for knives, where little modification was needed. A bone flute made from an eagle's wing-bone comes from Hedeby. The Trondheim pin is an outstanding example of such bone-working (78).

Whalebone, some of which was scavenged from mammals which had died along the coasts, was another material with great potential because of its size. Two whalebone plaques from northern Norway, used as ironing or linen-smoothing boards, and carved with striking openwork terminals, are outstanding examples (36). Another from a rich female grave at Birka shows how prized they were. From northern Norway comes a particularly fine line-winder used in fishing (25) and other tools such as weaving-swords of whalebone.

77 *Fragment of an unfinished tenth-century grave-slab found at Coppergate, York.*

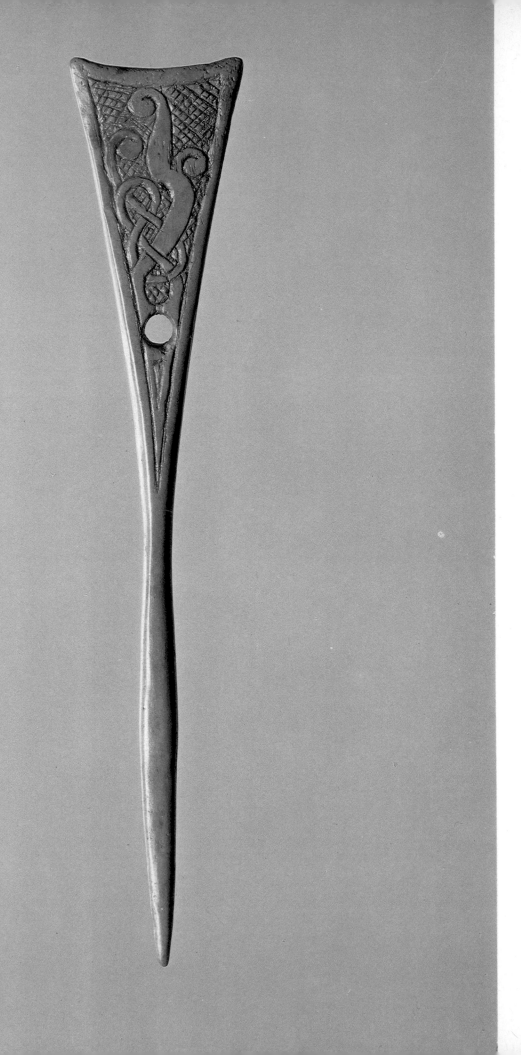

78 *A bone pin lightly incised with an eleventh-century Urnes-style animal, from Trondheim.*

Sophisticated and professional working of antler occurred on all urban sites. Where evidence exists it suggests that antlers of the red deer were normally gathered after being shed, rather than being taken from hunted animals. They must have been traded to the towns by the country-dwellers of the hinterlands. Many different kinds of artefacts were made from antler, skilfully and economically utilising its naturally occurring shapes and contours, to use as much of their raw material as possible. A whole series of fine tools would have been necessary to undertake delicate work, as in making composite pieces, especially combs. The long comb is a characteristically Viking artefact and, although varying in detail and form, was constructed on very similar lines in towns as diverse as Trondheim and Hedeby. A pair of long plates ran the length either side to form the back of the comb, between which were riveted a series of rectangular tablets; into these the fine teeth were cut. The teeth were sometimes protected by a composite comb-case, which could be worn suspended, as the example from York. Waste material from the processes of manufacture abounds on urban sites, especially resulting from failure to saw the teeth of the comb successfully.

Zoomorphic art of the highest order occurs on the finest antler work. The antler and bronze casket from Cammin, lost in the war, had large outer decorative panels carved with Mammen-style ornament. The lower guard from a sword-hilt found at Sigtuna is a classic expression of the style (98) and also exemplifies a specialised range of fittings manufactured at Birka. The carved elk-antler fitting from Sigtuna, perhaps from a casket, which terminates in a man's head, stands at the peak of this art (64).

Antler was also used for making tools, such as a light hammer-head from Birka, perhaps used in fine gold-work. It can be seen in the jaws of a clamp from Hedeby to hold delicate antler or fine metal during the finishing of an object. Antler moulds for casting ornaments, and dies for impressing gold or bronze foil, form a link to another complex of craft activities – that of fine metalworking. For not only did the Vikings adapt imported items such as coins or mounts for costume jewellery, but developed their craftsmanship to the highest standard in creating a range of jewellery and ornamented vessels from imported metals – bronze, silver and gold.

10 The Jeweller's Craft

The gaudy ornaments so loved by the Scandinavian men and women of the Viking Age were produced by jewellers expert in many skills. That their achievements still command our admiration and respect rests on the excellence of their design and the technical mastery that they display. Many of the techniques of the Viking-Age jewellers can now only be imagined, but it is possible to reconstruct some of the processes they used. These appear not to have been very different from those recorded in the Middle Ages and are techniques that are much the same as those practised by traditional craftsmen today.

Jewellers' workshops are known from pre-Viking Scandinavia at Helgö in Sweden, where there was mass-production of bronze brooches cast in clay moulds. The Helgö excavations have shown that the activities of early Viking-Age metalworkers at places like Ribe, Kaupang, Birka and Hedeby were no new development, although the standardisation of much Viking-Age jewellery, and its wide distribution, suggests that much greater mass-production developed during this period.

Coins, ingots or scrap-metal were melted in small crucibles on charcoal hearths, heated by bellows. The bellows would have been made of skin and wood so that it is not surprising that they do not survive. However, bellows had to be protected from the furnace by a guard fitted over the end of the nozzle. Soapstone was much favoured for this purpose and these bellows-guards could be ornamented, although rarely as interestingly as the one found on the beach at Snaptun in Jutland (46).

Crucibles had to be made of fine clay and the best-quality ones were imported from the Rhineland. The poor clay available for locally made crucibles was often less well-suited for that purpose, as it reacted badly with the molten metal, producing a heavily encrusted appearance on use (79). When the metal had melted, the crucibles were lifted from the fire by means of long-handled iron tongs (71) so that the contents could be poured directly into the moulds of clay or stone. These were generally made in two parts, lashed together in use, with a funnel-like opening at the top, through which the metal could enter (79).

The majority of moulds were made with the design impressed by means of a specially prepared model or, more simply, by a finished object. For more elaborate objects the *cire-perdue*, or 'lost-wax', technique was used. In this method a model is made from wax and surrounded with clay to form the mould; it is then heated, so melting the wax, which is poured away to leave the mould empty and ready to receive the molten metal. Such moulds have to be broken to remove the cast object when cold. Stone moulds are also known (79). Soapstone was often chosen for open moulds

79 *Dragon's head mould from Birka, with moulds of stone and antler from Hedeby, and crucible from Lund.*

for casting ingots, or other simple objects such as Thor's hammers and cross-pendants. Also found at Hedeby are moulds carved from antler which were used for the mass-production of cheap brooches of pewter, an alloy of tin and lead (79). Experiment has shown that these seemingly fragile forms could have been reused repeatedly without suffering damage.

After casting, the objects would have been filed and polished to remove casting seams and other flaws, and then further decoration might be applied by means of a graver or punch. On the other hand, many mould-fragments show that the finely detailed ornament was reproduced during casting, only needing to be tidied up afterwards (this will have been the case with many of the silver and bronze objects illustrated). Engraving was, nevertheless, much practised in the Viking Age, often with great skill, as may be seen on the gilt-bronze vanes from Heggen and Söderala (9, 99), or the silver bowl from Lilla Valla on Gotland (105).

Punching and stamping were also favourite Viking-Age methods of decorating metalwork. Punches are simply blunt-ended metal rods, struck with a hammer to form depressions in the surface of the metal; they can, however, be engraved with simple patterns to form decorative stamps. Many silver arm-rings have only punched ornament for decoration (80); particularly favoured motifs were based on triangles, often arranged in hour-glass form. A punch like that formed part of the equipment of the Mästermyr craftsman, together with a lead stamping-pad. Punching and stamping were also combined with other types of ornament, for instance, on the borders and animal bodies of some of the Broa mounts (88), or as the background to the engraved ornament on the vanes (9, 99), and Lilla Valla bowl (105).

This fluted bowl from Lilla Valla was hammered up from sheet-metal, rather than being cast. Other relatively simple objects, such as band-shaped arm-rings, were also hammered out from cast ingots, as were the large rods that were made for plaiting and twisting into rings of all sizes (81). Thus hammers of various dimensions and types were important tools for Viking-Age craftsmen; they ranged from the heavy sledge-hammers of the blacksmith (72), to very light ones which were intended for jewellers' use, such as the one made of elk-antler from Birka. Gold and silver foils which were hammered out and stamped with dies were used in a variety of ways. Foils like those from Hauge (41), for example, may be complete in themselves, but during the Viking Age embossed foils were more often used to support elaborate filigree work of the type described below. The solid bronze die from Mammen, with its stylised animal ornament, would have been used for just such a purpose (82).

It is difficult today to imagine fully the effects that Viking-Age jewellers would have achieved on their newly finished objects. Burial destroys the surface appearance of bronzes which take on patinas ranging from leather-brown to olive-green. The jewellers probably knew how to create such effects, but one imagines that bronze was generally used in an unpatinated state to show off its golden colour; this has been re-created on a few pieces, like the Asen brooch (53). Gilding was used on the finest silver and bronze objects (the Broa mounts and Heggen vane, for example; 87, 99), either to

80 ABOVE LEFT *Elaborately stamped silver arm-ring from Sweden.*

81 BELOW LEFT *A gold arm-ring from Virginia, Ireland.*

82 BELOW *Tenth-century metalworker's die, from Mammen, for impressing metal foils.*

create the impression that the object was actually made of gold, or simply to introduce a contrasting colour into the over-all decorative scheme. Several gilding techniques were in use, and mercury, used in the fire-gilding process, has been excavated at Hedeby. Other bronze objects were coated in white metal (generally tin) to provide cheap imitations for ordinary men and women of the silver ornaments worn by rich and fashionable Vikings.

Silver itself was applied to the surface of base metal objects in a number of different ways: by means of thin plates, by encrustation (when silver is hammered on to a hatched surface), or by inlay (where wires are hammered into engraved lines). The two latter methods were the ones used to ornament the Viking warrior's finest iron equipment, from sword-hilts (62, 83) to stirrups and spurs, the silver being contrasted with copper and brass to form elaborate multi-coloured patterns. Objects of silver, or those encrusted with silver, were often engraved with patterns that were inlaid with a pure black substance known as 'niello' – usually silver sulphide; its blackness provided the perfect contrast to the silver surface (e.g. 100).

Further surface enrichment was provided by the addition of filigree and granulation, and on rare occasions by the use of semi-precious stones or glass inlays. Gem-setting had been an extremely popular form of ornament in pre-Viking Scandinavia, when it had been practised most skilfully. It was clearly not to Viking taste and was to all intents and purposes abandoned. There is a slip of garnet used for the eye of a horse-shaped brooch from Birka (56), and a single setting of glass at the centre of the Rinkaby brooch (91). One might also point to the five (empty) settings on one of the two great Hornelund disc brooches (57). These instances are only notable for their rarity.

The Hornelund brooches provide superb examples of filigree and granulation work. Filigree consists of fine gold or silver wires, either plain or worked to look like a miniature string of beads, soldered to the surface being ornamented. It is often combined with granulation – small balls or grains of metal used either in clusters or singly (then often with a collar of beaded filigree wire). Both can be seen in simple form on the gold pendant from Ringome (54), or the silver Thor's hammer from Bredsätra (44). Plain filigree wire could be made using draw-plates (iron sheets with series of graded holes), as found at both Bygland and Mästermyr (71). A hammered-out rod of gold or silver would be drawn by tongs through these plates a number of times, until it was reduced to the required thickness.

Objects entirely decorated with gold filigree and granulation, such as the Hedeby brooches and pendants (84) show how skilled some Scandinavian jewellers were in these techniques; the Nonnebakken and Tråen disc brooches demonstrate the same in silver (95). Another use was on bronze objects, when filigree and granulation were sometimes used in combination with other forms of decoration, as on the ends of the Møllerløkken brooch (60). In such cases the filigree had to be soldered on to a base-plate of foil which was then fitted into the object. These foils

83 RIGHT *Sword-hilt from the Hedeby boat-burial, encrusted with silver and inlaid with niello.*

84 OVERLEAF LEFT *Gold brooches and pendants with filigree and granulation, found at Hedeby.*

85 OVERLEAF RIGHT *Masterpiece of Gotlandic jewellery: a bronze brooch embellished with gold, silver and niello.*

could be embossed to provide raised platforms for more ambitious patterns, in the manner used on the top and sides of the Mårtens brooch (85).

86 'Trial-pieces' from the Dublin excavations.

Such pieces illustrate the skills of the Viking-Age jeweller better than words, but the jeweller was more than just a highly skilled craftsman; he would have been his own designer – often a true artist. Nowhere is this better demonstrated in the Viking world than in Dublin. Recent excavations of the Viking-Age town have produced a remarkable assortment of so-called 'trial-pieces' (86). These are animal-bones, and occasionally stones, on which a wide variety of patterns has been carved – consisting of stylised animals and interlace motifs inspired by the tenth- and eleventh-century Scandinavian art-styles described in the next chapter. The exact purpose of these designs is unknown. Some are clearly practice pieces on which an artist has tried out new patterns; some may have been used for training apprentices. Others have fully finished designs and could have been used for impressing wax models for use in making moulds, or even in the manner of modern pattern-books to attract prospective customers.

Dublin was clearly an artistic centre of importance and the widespread impact of Scandinavian art-styles on the native art of Ireland, in the eleventh and twelfth centuries, must be ascribed to this influence. Skilled craftsmen anywhere would have chosen to be based in towns, where they would have been readily accessible to their patrons and where their materials would have been available. Others concerned with mass-production would equally have preferred to be urban based, selling their wares to middlemen for distribution in the countryside. Yet others would have travelled, seeking commissions where they could find them.

The maker of any object was known as a smith, whether silversmith or iron-smith. To many Vikings the weapon-smith was most important of all such craftsmen, but the rich inheritance left by their artists and jewellers is likely to place them first in our modern estimation.

11 Art and Ornament

Vigour and vitality imbue the best of the Vikings' art; in this respect their art could be seen as a direct reflection of their character. Its intricacy and complexity were characteristics shared by Scandinavian poetry of the Viking Age. But by the end of the period, their art developed a smooth elegance that is almost decadent in its refinement, at a time when the outward energy of the Vikings seems to have been spent.

Viking art is based throughout on animal forms, in a tradition that can be traced back to the art of the Late Roman Empire. At the same time it is limited in that it was largely a decorative art, applied to a wide variety of objects used in daily life. One should not belittle its quality on this account, for the Vikings loved ornament and valued the artist's skills. But the result is that Viking art is difficult for the modern student to appreciate, except by careful study of its conventions. This can, however, be a rewarding experience, for it remains one direct approach to the spirit of the age. If in the end its contents escape our understanding, we may yet retain deep admiration for its quality and technical skill, and for the culture that produced it.

Animals in many guises form the main motifs of Viking art. A continuous development in the treatment of their contorted and convoluted bodies can be traced throughout the Viking Age, so helping to define its changing art-styles. This obsession with stylised animals as a basis for ornament had its roots in the last days of the Roman Empire. Motifs were borrowed by Germanic artists from late Roman provincial art, but attempts at naturalism were rapidly rejected in Scandinavia. During the fifth to eighth centuries over much of the Germanic world (including Anglo-Saxon England), the original animal and human figures became increasingly disjointed and distorted, with results that are unintelligible to the inexperienced eye. The same is true for much of Viking art, but it can be deciphered with patience and practice. The initial impression is of chaos, often brilliant and dramatic, but underneath the crowded surfaces are carefully controlled schemes of ornament using standardised, but changing motifs. Viking art was self-assured and little affected by that of the rest of Europe until the end of the eleventh century, except for borrowing occasional motifs or patterns; but finally it succumbed to the Romanesque art of western Europe.

Throughout these pages are illustrations of weapons, brooches and tools, all elaborately decorated as, indeed, are all the finest Viking artefacts, be they ships or churches, tent-posts or tombstones. The ornament often covers the whole available surface, for there was an ostentatious and flashy aspect to the Viking character that we find realised

87 Gilt bronze bridle-mounts from Broa: a Gotlandic masterpiece from the beginning of the Viking Age.

in much of their jewellery and other personal possessions. Viking art is thus decorative or applied art on functional objects. There is little representational art, and that which exists is probably of cult significance, like the little figure from Rällinge (40). Such figures demonstrate that Scandinavian artists were capable of a more naturalistic approach when it suited them (compare the Sigtuna warrior's head; 64), but it clearly had little appeal to the spirit of the age. In this respect an artist's sketches or doodles, such as those on stone from Jarlshof in Shetland (7a), or Löddeköppinge in Sweden (7b), are all the more revealing and important for their rarity.

Most of the finest surviving pieces from the early Viking Age have been found in graves, but later Viking art is best represented on objects from silver hoards and on the incised stones erected to commemorate good deeds or dead men (e.g. 105, 101). But the sad truth is that we are missing most of the greatest achievements of the Viking-Age artists, for their natural medium must have been wood which has long since rotted away. From the beginning of the Viking Age there survives a magnificent series of carved wooden objects, once sealed in the great Oseberg ship-burial in south-east Norway. The Oseberg ship itself, the wagon, sledges, and many other pieces are all richly carved with amazing skill in the earliest Viking style by a group of gifted artists working under royal patronage. Preserved from the late Viking Age is the remarkable portal of a wooden church at Urnes in western Norway (115), incorporated into its twelfth-century successor. The artistry and skilled craftsmanship demonstrated on these examples of wood-carving tantalise us and excite our admiration and appreciation, for otherwise our knowledge of Scandinavian wood-carving from the Viking Age would be dependent on the chance survival of fragments, such as those from Flatatunga in Iceland (114) or that recently excavated in Trondheim, Norway.

There are, however, a few small-scale carvings in other materials – amber (74), jet (16), bone (97), and walrus ivory (75) – to remind us both of the skills of the Scandinavian sculptor and of how well suited his Viking Age animal motifs were to this purpose. It seems strange in this case that stone-carving was neglected in Scandinavia until the later tenth century, except on Gotland where there alone existed an earlier tradition. Even then one can hardly say of these Gotlandic 'picture-stones' (e.g. 8, 47) that they use to the full the possibilities of stone as an artistic medium; the slabs dating from the beginning of the Viking Age are often finely shaped in themselves, but only to serve as flat surfaces for lightly incised scenes which are the nearest that Viking art came to being narrative. The most popular motif is a ship under sail, often with a fully armed crew (e.g. Smiss, with its helmeted, shield-bearing warriors; 8), while others also portray events (e.g. Lillbjärs, 47) in a manner similar to that on a tapestry found in the Oseberg ship-burial – another medium employed by Scandinavian artists during the Viking Age of which we now know almost nothing. Occasionally individual figures of men and women are found in metalwork, dressed and posed in the same manner as those on the 'picture-stones' and the tapestry.

88 TOP and Fig. 9 ABOVE
*The main motifs of the Broa
mounts.*

The meaning of such scenes and figures is generally lost, for we lack the contemporary documents that might have explained them to us. It is speculation to identify them with the pagan gods and heroic deeds described in later literary sources, although occasionally identifications can be made with some certainty, as on the Kirk Andreas stone (49). But for the most part we have to admit that the significance of such narrative scenes and semi-naturalistic figures (including that, if any, of the animal-ornament) is lost, or at best obscure.

The beginning of the Viking Age is not marked by the sudden appearance of a new art-style, but saw the continuation of one that was current in the eighth century, with the addition of one new and highly significant motif. This earliest Viking art-style, as found at Oseberg, is difficult to date, but it was clearly most popular at the end of the eighth century and during the early part of the ninth. It employs three main motifs which can be conveniently described from their use on a series of gilt-bronze bridle-mounts, found in a man's grave at Broa on Gotland. These twenty-two mounts (87) have been described as 'one of the most brilliant series of objects of the Scandinavian Viking Age' and of a technical quality 'as fine as that of any collection of metalwork known from contemporary Europe'. Despite the variety in their designs, they are clearly the product of a single workshop – most probably of one man, active on Gotland in the early ninth century.

The design of the mounts themselves, with their use of geometric frameworks, should be considered before the actual motifs are looked at in detail. In some cases these frameworks divide the surface so that one animal fills each of the fields; alternatively a framework may be superimposed over an animal (e.g. 88) which then appears to be behind an openwork screen. In other instances the animals are superimposed on the framework, which is gripped by them with their paws. Whatever the approach chosen by the Broa master the framework was carefully designed by him to be more than just a border; it is intimately related to the variety and composition of the animal-ornament itself.

The first motif to note is the elongated animal viewed in profile (fig. 9a; see ill. 88); it has a sinuous double-contoured body, with a small head, a prominent eye and a frond-like pigtail. The body is pierced at the neck and hip by heart-shaped openings through which tendrils are threaded. The second motif is an animal more compact than the first, lacking its double contour (fig. 9b; see ill. 87). In other respects it is very similar to the first motif, although it often takes the form of a bird; some of those conceived by the Broa master have splendidly puffed-up breasts. The third motif is the 'gripping beast' (fig. 9c; see ill. 87).

'Gripping beasts' take their name from their most obvious characteristic – the paws that grip the frames around or under them, that grip themselves, or even each other (several beasts may be interlocked together in compositions resembling wild mêlées). These vigorous animals are the new invention in Scandinavian art. They appealed so greatly to Viking taste that they enjoyed wide popularity and even survived as a motif into the tenth century. They took many forms during this period, from the low

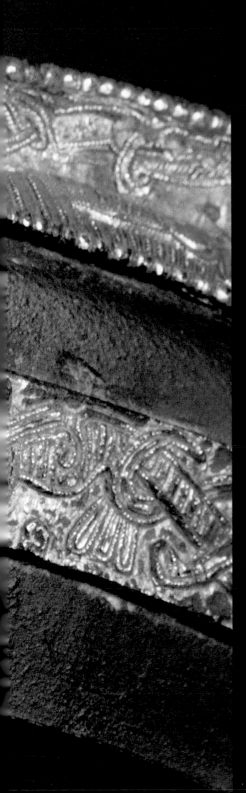

89 *The animal-head terminal
of the Mammen horse-collar
(detail of 28).*

90 ABOVE AND RIGHT *Gilt bronze mounts from the Norwegian ship-burials at Borre (a, b) and Gokstad (c).*

91 OVERLEAF LEFT *Gilt silver brooch from Rinkaby, Sweden, ornamented with Borre-style 'gripping-beasts'.*

92 OVERLEAF RIGHT *Reconstructed ninth-century necklace of beads and pendants, from Hon in Norway.*

relief of the Broa mounts (88) and the Steinsvik sword-hilt (62), to those arising in openwork from the Asen brooch (53), from the three-dimensional pair in jet from Tresfjorden (16), to that tucked into the mouth of the animal-headed terminal on a horse-collar from Mammen in Denmark (89).

As the ninth century progressed, this earliest Viking-Age style was succeeded by two new styles, both of which are named after places in Scandinavia where important ornamented objects were found. The first of these to emerge was the Borre style, so-called from a rich barrow-burial at Borre in Vestfold, Norway. The grave-goods included a bridle lavishly ornamented with gilt-bronze mounts (90), but quite different in style to those from Broa and, incidentally, of lesser quality. These Borre mounts are not the most exciting examples of the style which bears their name, but they are among the most typical.

The new motif of importance in the Borre style was the 'ring-chain' – an interlace pattern made up of a double ribbon bound by a series of rings surrounding hollow-sided lozenges (90a). It was also adapted to form a simple knot. This Borre ring-chain often terminated in an animal-mask. Such masks formed an important feature of the style, consisting of triangular faces with protruding, 'Mickey Mouse-type' ears, like those of the animals on the Asen brooch (53).

Heads like these were often used for the gripping beasts that were the second main motif of the Borre style. Borre-style gripping beasts occur singly in a characteristic posture, with a ribbon-like body arranged in an arc beneath the head, and with paws that grip its own body and the frame around it. They are clearly seen on a silver-gilt brooch from Rinkaby in Sweden (91). Once the Rinkaby ornament is understood, then so can the animals on a silver disc brooch from Nonnebakken in Denmark (95).

The third main motif found on the Borre mounts is a simple backward-looking animal, stylised as usual, but of naturalistic proportions (90b). This design is rare in the Borre style, but occurs in a different form on a series of mounts from the Gokstad ship-burial (90c). Among the Gokstad mounts are also some unusually naturalistic roundels, depicting spear-carrying horsemen.

The Borre style is seen at its best in rare examples of filigree work, but many cast objects in this style illustrate the trick of using nicked lines to imitate the appearance of beaded filigree wires; for example, the Borre and Gokstad mounts (90). A three-dimensional version of the style flourished in central Sweden and Russia, with animal figures in the round that are distantly related to the backward-looking ones on the Borre mounts.

The Borre style had developed by the middle of the ninth century, as is shown by the fact that some pendants in this style (already old) were apparently mounted with a few coins to form a necklace in about 855–860. These various pendants form part of the Hon hoard from Norway, the largest gold hoard known from Viking Age Scandinavia; the necklace as shown here consists of a modern selection of pieces from this rich find (92).

The Borre style was very popular throughout Scandinavia and in the areas of Scandinavian settlement in Russia, where the pendants in the

hoard from Vårby, Sweden, may have been made (93). Its influence was felt to a lesser extent in Britain and Ireland; the ring-chain appears on stone sculpture in the north of England and on the Isle of Man (49), but also in other materials, such as a bone trial-piece from the Dublin excavations (86), and a wooden gaming-board (39) from Ireland.

The Borre style did not go out of fashion until the second half of the tenth century, so that for much of its life it was contemporary with the so-called 'Jellinge style', which was popular from the late ninth until the late tenth century. One need not be surprised then that the two styles are occasionally found on the same object. The metalworker's die from Mammen in Denmark, for instance, combines Jellinge-style animals with Borre-style interlace (82).

The Jellinge style, so called from the ornament of a small silver cup found in the Danish royal burial-mound at Jelling in Jutland (69), has as its chief motif an animal with a ribbon-shaped body, such as those which ornament the horse-collars from the same grave as the Mammen die (28). These animals can be seen more clearly on one of the pendants (93) from the Vårby hoard, which was buried about 940. The S-shaped body is a double-contoured ribbon; the head is shown in profile, with a long pigtail and a curlicue on the upper lip; the hip is often marked by a spiral. Such ribbon-like bodies presumably descend from the Borre-style gripping

93 BELOW *Pendants from the Vårby hoard display both ribbon-shaped animals of the Jellinge style and a Borre-style 'gripping-beast'.*

beasts (as on other pendants in the Vårby hoard), while the layout of the animal is familiar from the early Viking Age. The Jellinge style is thus very much 'in the mainstream of Scandinavian art'.

The Jellinge style was introduced into England by Scandinavian settlers who found there an art that was also based on highly stylised animals and which in fact went back to common Germanic origins. In the north-east they encountered stone sculpture for the first time. They rapidly adopted for their own use the Anglo-Saxon tradition of memorial crosses which were often decorated with animal ornament. An unfinished grave-slab from York (77) shows the standard that tenth-century Anglo-Scandinavian sculptors could achieve in a metropolitan centre, by drawing on the Jellinge style for inspiration.

Yet elsewhere in Britain the Jellinge style was practised with skill and originality. The terminals of some silver brooches, concealed in about 950 as part of a large hoard at Skaill, on Orkney, are engraved with very late Jellinge-style ornament (fig. 10; see ill. 94), paralleled in stone sculpture on some Viking crosses in the Isle of Man. Here again are to be seen the vigorous and assertive qualities of all that is best in Viking art. The late feature of the Skaill ornament is the tendency for leaf-like tendrils to sprout from various parts of the design, giving it a florid quality more characteristic of the following Mammen style.

94 RIGHT and Fig. 10 ABOVE
Silver brooch-terminal from the Skaill hoard, on Orkney, ornamented with a Jellinge-style beast.

Familiarity with the animal-ornament of the Jellinge style should make it possible to take up the challenge presented by such objects as a silver disc brooch from the Tråen hoard, buried in Norway during the last decade of the tenth century. This filigree-ornamented brooch (95a) is in the same tradition as the Borre-style brooch from Nonnebakken, already noted (95b), with the animals translated into the Jellinge style. The initial impression is one of a writhing mass of worms, like disturbed ground-bait, with little or no aesthetic appeal. Yet fun can be had in disentangling the animals that make up the composition, which is the same as that on the Nonnebakken brooch (although Tråen uses only three animals to the latter's four). The animals are in profile with the normal Jellinge-style features.

To identify a head, start at the centre of the brooch and pick out the large silver granule that forms its eye, with the upper-lip curlicue before it; the elongated pigtail which sprouts above it may then be followed as a ribbon, interlacing in and out of the parts of the neighbouring animal. Its neck and body are formed by similar ribbons, arranged in the manner of the Nonnebakken Borre-style beasts – forequarters to the right and hind-

95a, b *Silver disc brooches from Norway and Denmark, ornamented* ABOVE *in the Jellinge style and* RIGHT *Borre style.*

quarters to the left (with a tail). A single limb emerges from each joint, terminating in a foot represented by a U-shaped element. In the end, every strand will be seen to have its place in a balanced composition. If the over-all impression is one of restlessness, it could be said that this is another facet of the Viking character to emerge in their art.

The Mammen style developed directly from the Jellinge style with the result that it is occasionally difficult to tell them apart, as with the ornament on the Skaill brooches. They were in any case contemporary for a while, as the Mammen style was in fashion during the second half of the tenth century and the very beginning of the eleventh. It is a style that was particularly suited to carving and is most frequently found in stone, ivory and bone.

The fully developed Mammen style is easily recognisable. The Mammen animal is a more substantial version of the Jellinge beast, with the addition of fleshy plant tendrils, based on the acanthus-leaf ornament so popular in western European art of the tenth century. For the first time in Viking art we see a substantial use of plant motifs, both as surrounds for animal ornament and, to a lesser extent, in their own right. The animals

themselves are no longer so ribbon-like, but have more naturalistic proportions. Double-contouring continues and the bodies are filled with beading or billets; the hip-spiral is more strongly emphasised.

The style takes its name from a silver inlaid axe found at Mammen in Jutland (but not from the same grave as the other Mammen pieces described before). The most important object in this style comes from Jutland, the royal memorial at Jelling with its runic inscription telling that it was erected by King Harald 'Bluetooth'; this dates it to between 965 and 985. Two faces of this pyramidal stone (96) are ornamented, one with a stylised representation of the Crucifixion, and the other with a large, four-legged lion-like beast entwined in the coils of a snake. This may well be the first Viking-Age stone sculpture to have been erected in southern Scandinavia.

The two subjects displayed on the Jelling stone are both new to Scandinavian art and, taken together with the introduction of foliate patterns, show that the Mammen style represents a phase not only of continuity but also of innovation. Firstly, the figure of Christ testifies to the introduction of Christianity and to the copying of European models (seen also in the acanthus motifs). Secondly, the 'great beast' motif (combined with its snake or serpent) marks a new stage in the development of Viking art, for a single animal had not previously been used in this way to create a full composition. Other finds, however, show Mammen-style animals used in the traditional way, as elements of a larger composition, such as on a cylindrical bone mount from Årnes in Norway (fig. 11; see ill. 97), or on some of the Manx crosses.

The Jelling stone presents a very formalised version of the Mammen style, but this royal monument seems to have set the fashion for stone memorials in southern Scandinavia and eventually further afield, for we see a similar scene of a 'great beast' on a stone from St Paul's, London (101), executed in the succeeding Ringerike style. The most vivacious examples of Mammen-style motifs can be found on two caskets. One of walrus ivory was formerly in the Bamberg Cathedral treasury (now in the Bavarian National Museum at Munich). The other was very similar in

96 LEFT *The Jelling stone: the royal memorial erected by King Harald 'Bluetooth' of Denmark to his parents and himself.*

97 BELOW and fig. 11 RIGHT *Carved bone mount from Årnes in Norway, with Mammen-style ornament of three interlacing animals.*

style, but far larger and with antler panels. It was preserved in the treasury of Cammin Cathedral in Pomerania, but was destroyed in the Second World War. Also in antler is a sword-guard from the early Swedish town of Sigtuna, finely ornamented with Mammen-style motifs having some Ringerike-style elements (98). The Mammen style at its best displays an exuberance not seen in Viking art before. This exuberance is carried over into the Ringerike style, which grew out of it, although the latter is more disciplined in its design.

The Ringerike style is so called after the geological name for the sandstone beds in the Oslo region of Norway which provided the material for a small number of finely ornamented slabs. Western European influences are again felt in this style, plant-ornament gaining ground at the expense of the animals. The latter were liable to be subordinated to clusters of elongated tendrils, such as the classic examples on the gilt-bronze vane from Heggen in Norway (99), springing from the head and tail of the 'great beast'. A row of similar tendrils forms the outer border to the composition. A vane from Söderala Church in Sweden is a brilliant example of the late Ringerike style, with its strong and direct appeal.

A most elegant and classic design of Ringerike-style lobes and tendrils is engraved on the Flatatunga panels from Iceland (114), while another version of them can be seen in gold filigree on one of the disc brooches from the Hornelund hoard, Denmark (57).

As illustrated by the Heggen and Söderala vanes, the three main motifs of the Ringerike style are thus: elongated tendrils (often with the addition of lobes), the 'great beast' and a snake (with the latter two often engaged in a conflict). They can all appear separately. Examples of Ringerike tendril patterns have just been noted, but they were put to many uses, as witness the treatment of Christ's hands on one of the two crucifixes found in a silver hoard, hidden in about 1035 in the Norwegian town of Trondheim (112).

The 'great beast' appears alone on top of the Heggen and Söderala vanes, cast in the round; in both cases it stands proudly on guard, staring out over the horizon. A further three-dimensional animal-head in this style forms one end of an arm-ring from Undrom in Sweden, which is in the form of a coiled snake, with rows of alternating tendrils and lobes inlaid in niello down its back (100). However, the principal use of a single snake in the Ringerike style was on Scandinavian runestones where its body was used to form the band that carries the runic inscription.

The Ringerike style proved particularly popular in England and Ireland where, in both cases, it possessed strong appeal for native artists. There are in fact few more successful expressions of the style than that on the end-slab of a stone box-tomb found in the churchyard of St Paul's Cathedral, London (101), described as 'one of the finest examples of Viking stone-carving known outside Gotland'. The 'great beast' has tendrils encircling its body, and a lesser beast around its front leg; lobes sprout from the upper corners of the field. The 'great beast' had a blue/black body covered in white spots and the stone still bears traces of the original paint. A design so uniquely Scandinavian, deriving ultimately from that on the Jelling stone,

98 *Mammen-style patterns cover both sides of the lower guard of a sword-hilt carved from elk-antler, found at Sigtuna.*

99 LEFT *The 'great beast'
strides majestically across the
Heggen vane (reverse of 9).*

could only have been executed in England during the period of Scandinavian domination (1014–42), most probably for one of the followers of Knut 'the Great'.

In Ireland the Ringerike style was widely adopted. The fashion will have been set in Dublin, where one of the recently excavated bone trial-pieces bears a design of looped Ringerike-style animals (102), recalling a fine disc brooch from Sweden, concealed about 1055 in a hoard at Gerete on Gotland (102). The design of the Dublin trial-piece (it uses two animals instead of the three at Gerete) appears in almost identical form on the gilt-bronze panels at either end of an Irish book-shrine – that of the *Cathac* – made in the late eleventh century.

As with all other Viking art-styles it is difficult to provide accurate dates for the beginning and end of the Ringerike style. It is clear that its period of high fashion was during the first half of the eleventh century, but in

101 LEFT *A 'great beast' and serpent fill the end-slab of a Scandinavian tomb from St Paul's Churchyard, London.*

102 ABOVE *Silver disc brooch with interlaced animals from an eleventh-century Gotlandic hoard.*

Ireland it remained popular until later. Its origins in the Mammen style lie presumably in the late tenth century.

An early tendency noted in the Ringerike style was the elongation of Mammen tendrils. This process of refinement was one that continued throughout the development of the style, leading eventually to the emergence of a new and ultimate Viking style. This was the Urnes style, which may have developed in Sweden where many transitional pieces have been found, both in stone and metalwork. Swedish sculptors and rune-masters, having finally taken up the idea of stone memorials, set to work in an experimental vein bringing their art to a high point with the Urnes style. There can be few finer illustrations of their achievements than the rectangular tomb from Ardre churchyard on Gotland (48).

The Urnes style, however, takes its name from the decoration of a small church that was built about 1060, on a remote farm at Urnes in western Norway. Parts of the original Urnes Church were reused in its twelfth-

century successor, which still stands today, and to this we owe the survival of a true masterpiece (115). Fragments of wood ornamented in the Urnes style are known from elsewhere, such as Trondheim, but there is nothing else, even in stone or metalwork, to prepare us for the brilliant artistry of the Urnes sculptor with his dramatic compositions and, on the west portal, almost three-dimensional relief. This is a further reminder of the wealth of Viking wood-carving that must have been lost to us.

The Urnes master ornamented the west portal with a composition created from three animal motifs whose gently swelling and tapering bodies, interlaced with narrow lines, form an undulating design. These three Urnes-style motifs are refinements of Mammen and Ringerike beasts: four-legged animals of greyhound-like proportions, a serpent-like animal with a single foreleg, and snakes that are but thin ribbons with animal-heads. The animals interlace together, biting each other in a 'combat' motif that is transformed from its Ringerike predecessor. Everywhere a new delicacy and elegance may be observed, particularly in the treatment of animal-heads, with their huge pointed eyes, their curlicued upper-lips and downward curled lower jaws. Plant motifs are less frequent than in the Ringerike style, but are not abandoned altogether.

A similar motif forms the basis for a series of openwork brooches; on some one animal with a single foreleg and a tapering body splitting into two is entwined with a snake (as for example, the brooch from the Danish settlement of Lindholm Høje; 103). Such brooches are known throughout Scandinavia and were certainly being produced in Lund in the early twelfth century. A related brooch in the form of a bird (104) was concealed as part of a Norwegian silver hoard at Gresli in about 1085. It is an early Urnes piece (the motif and certain details are carried over from the Ringerike style), as is the ornament on the beautiful bowl from the Lilla Valla hoard, buried on Gotland about 1050. The restrained use of ornament on this fluted bowl gives it an immediate appeal to all who otherwise find Viking art over-elaborate. Around its rim runs a frieze of animals, linked by pear-shaped lobes, and within it on the base is a single interlaced animal (105).

Such finds as the Lilla Valla bowl, and evidence of manufacturing from Lund allow the Urnes style in Scandinavia to be dated to the period between about 1040 and 1140. In Ireland it may have lingered on longer as the Ringerike style before it did.

The animals on the Lilla Valla bowl, with their sinuous bodies, single forelegs and split tails, have already been noted as characteristic of the Urnes style. The same beast appears in England on an openwork disc brooch found in the churchyard at Pitney, Somerset (106), where it forms part of the familiar 'combat' motif. In fact, the Urnes style is rare in southern England (in contrast to the Ringerike style), but there appears to have been a northern school of which the recently excavated mount from Lincoln provides a good example (106).

In Ireland the Urnes style caught the native imagination as the Ringerike had done earlier. The best-known piece in the Irish Urnes style is undoubtedly the Cross of Cong, dated by inscription to about 1123.

103 ABOVE LEFT *Openwork brooch in the form of a stylised beast, excavated at Lindholm Høje.*

104 BELOW LEFT *A bird-shaped brooch of gilt silver from an eleventh-century Norwegian hoard.*

Preserved in Boher Church, County Offaly, is a large gabled shrine of St Manchan (107) richly ornamented with metalwork; it has a central cross with boss-shaped ends and is covered with Urnes-style animals, which suggest that the two pieces were made in the same workshop. An unusual feature of this shrine is the series of half-round human figures on its front. The shrine is undated, but must be contemporary with the Cross of Cong. Other Irish objects suggest that the style continued to be used into the third quarter of the eleventh century.

In Ireland, as in Scandinavia, this last Viking art-style gradually waned although elements of the native tradition could still be found in Scandinavian folk-art until recent times. The world of the Vikings had undergone a complete transformation. The independence and self-confidence of the Vikings' art was lost and it finally succumbed to the pervasive influence of the Romanesque art of western Europe, as the Scandinavian nations were being drawn socially and politically into the brotherhood of Christian states.

105 ABOVE *Fluted silver bowl from Gotland with a gilded rim and interior roundel incised with intertwined animals.*

106 TOP RIGHT *A mount from Lincoln and* CENTRE RIGHT *a brooch from Pitney display the English Urnes style at its best.*

107 BOTTOM RIGHT *The gabled shrine of St Manchan is lavishly ornamented in twelfth-century Irish Urnes style.*

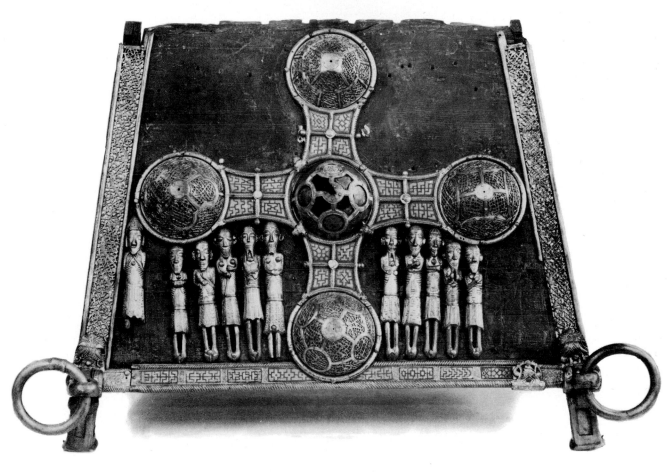

12 The Coming of Christianity

Helgi 'the Lean', a Viking settler of Iceland, is said to have 'believed in Christ and yet made vows to Thor for sea-voyages or in tight corners, and for everything which struck him as of real importance'. Helgi was certainly not alone in adding the Christian god to the ranks of his pagan ones. This was simple enough given the loosely organised nature of Norse belief. Even the first Christian missionaries did not attempt to deny the existence of the heathen gods, but reduced them to the role of demons.

The conversion of Scandinavia was a gradual process and so there was a considerable period of co-existence between pagans and Christians in the Viking world, with the addition of those of mixed beliefs to further confuse the picture. Is, for example, that Icelandic silver pendant from Foss (45) really a stylised hammer worn to invoke the protection of Thor? It is certainly made in the tradition of such pendants, with its animal-headed suspension-loop, as one can see by comparing it with that from Bredsätra (44), but it has been given a distinct cross-shape. So is it perhaps the sort of pendant that a man like Helgi might have worn to hedge his bets?

Contemporary sources describe both heathens and Christians living at Hedeby and Birka. To cater for the requirements of such mixed communities, metalworkers clearly had to be able to produce a variety of religious pendants. The jeweller whose mould was found at Trendgaarden in Denmark was a man of ingenuity and good business sense, as it was made for casting hammers and crosses at the same time.

The influence of Christianity is also revealed to archaeology by gradual changes in pagan Scandinavian burial practices. Cremation was abandoned (as of course was human sacrifice); then the burial of grave-goods died out. But all sorts of problems must have arisen from these changes. What was a heathen family to do with the body of a newly converted relation? How would Helgi have wished to be buried? Situations of these kinds may provide the explanations for a number of fully equipped Scandinavian burials found in churchyards in England and the Isle of Man – pagan rites on Christian sites. Or what of the enigma presented by the scene carved on the shaft of the cross from Middleton Church in Yorkshire (30)? It is often said to be a picture of the dead Viking in whose memory the cross was raised, like a warrior laid out in his grave with his weapons. To dispose of this apparent anomaly, it has been suggested instead that the scene shows a living man, seated in state and surrounded by his weapons, as symbols of his authority as a Viking leader.

The adoption of stone monuments as suitable memorials for the Christian dead, both in the British Isles and in Scandinavia, has already been mentioned. The Scandinavian runestones found in the countryside

108 *Enamelled Irish crozier-head from Helgö in Sweden.*

are not actual gravestones, but many are memorials raised to men and women buried elsewhere, for with the introduction of churchyards, the dead were no longer buried in the traditional cemeteries, located among the living. However, memorials might still be raised there. In some areas in the eleventh century we find churchyards dignified with stone box-tombs standing over the graves, in the same way as the house-shaped tomb-covers set up in the tenth century by Viking settlers and Anglo-Scandinavians in the north of England. Simple shaped slabs were also placed over Christian graves (sometimes with decorated stones at either end) and the Coppergate fragment found in the York excavations was apparently being carved for such a purpose when abandoned (77).

The finest stone box-tombs known are from Sweden, that from Ardre on Gotland (48) being high among them in the quality of its design and workmanship. The Urnes-style ornament dates this monument to the late eleventh century, while its runic inscription tells how it was erected by the sons of Liknat, to the memory of Ailikn, a good wife and mother. The St Paul's Churchyard stone from London (101) is from a similar type of monument, although its Ringerike-style ornament places it early in the eleventh century.

From the beginning of the Viking Age Scandinavians had direct contact with Christianity in several ways. Their raids on western Europe led to many Christians being captured as slaves. We hear of early missionaries to Denmark, like Archbishop Unni of Hamburg-Bremen (919–36), comforting Christian captives, while St Rimbert on a visit to Schleswig is said to have given his horse with its gear to free a fettered nun from a slave-gang. Of greater influence than the presence of Christian slaves in Scandinavia were the contacts with Christian merchants. Heathens wishing to do business with Christians had to receive the cross-mark, *prima signatio*, which was the first rite of initiation into the Christian Church. The tolerance and lack of organisation of Scandinavian paganism certainly hastened its collapse in the face of Christianity, but one is left wondering to what extent shrewd business sense lead to rapid conversions, particularly in those areas like England and Ireland where Scandinavians settled among Christian peoples. Merchants and mercenaries in the east will likewise have come into direct contact with Christianity in the form of the Orthodox religion of the Byzantine Eastern Empire and the Slav-Byzantine Church of South Russia (24).

The first Christian missionaries to Scandinavia were active in the eighth century in Denmark, but met with little success. The Helgö crosier-head (108) has been taken as evidence for an unrecorded mission, but one cannot be sure that this eighth-century Irish object arrived in the hands of a missionary. It could equally well have been loot taken on an early Viking raid.

The first successful apostle of Scandinavia was St Ansgar, a German monk, sent by the Emperor Louis the Pious on a mission that led him by way of Hedeby to Birka in 829 or 830, and then again about the middle of the century. But the work of Ansgar, who became the first Archbishop of Hamburg, later Hamburg-Bremen, and that of his followers in Sweden

had no lasting effect, although as a result Christians would have been tolerated for the most part. Such at least is suggested by a number of small crosses from the Birka graves, the finest of which is a small crucifix of silver (109) – an excellent example of tenth-century Scandinavian filigree-work.

The first Christians to be kings of Sweden reigned in the eleventh century, with the first bishop in the kingdom being established about 1050 in Sigtuna. The nobles and wealthy farmers among Sweden's converts of the eleventh century have left us many demonstrations of their faith in the form of cross-bearing runestones. Such stones commemorate their dead relations, or even themselves, by advertising their own good deeds. Such deeds took many forms, but the building of bridges is particularly often mentioned. These were generally causeways across marshland, or improved fords. Their construction was considered a suitably charitable act to benefit the builder's soul, or that of a relation, because it opened up access to churches and made it easier for priests to visit the sick and dying.

Among surviving inscriptions we can read, for instance, cut into a rock-face at Näs in Uppland that 'Livsten had the bridges made for his soul's health and for that of his sons, Jorund and Niklas and Luden'. Or elsewhere in Uppland, on a stone set up at Eggeby, that 'Ragnälv had this bridge made in memory of Anund, her good son. May God help his spirit and soul better than he deserved'.

Such inscriptions provide good evidence for the spread of Christianity in Sweden and as such are supported by several finds of silver crucifixes in eleventh- and early twelfth-century hoards. One from Gotland and one from Öland are illustrated (110, 111), both depicting Christ as bound (rather than nailed) to the cross. The former is cast and is rather coarse work, but the latter (which is in fact a hinged reliquary) is delicately incised and inlaid with niello.

The first Scandinavian country to be officially converted to Christianity was Denmark; King Harald's proud boast on the Jelling stone that it was he who had 'made the Danes Christian' stands as evidence. Harald became Christian himself between 960 and 965, although as early as 948 sees had been established at Hedeby, Ribe and Århus, with German missionary bishops sent by Hamburg-Bremen, the archdiocese founded with the purpose of bringing the faith to the north. By the early eleventh century there were also bishops at Odense and at Roskilde, with another in Skåne. Their number grew further in the eleventh century, but it was not until 1104 that the first Dane was consecrated as an archbishop, with his see based on Lund. Only then did the Scandinavian Church escape the domination of Hamburg-Bremen.

Ansgar had been able to build a church at Hedeby (although it was closed in the mid ninth century during a period of anti-Christian feeling, or perhaps because of indifference), but this and its successors must have been situated in an area of the town not as yet excavated. In comparison with Birka, the many graves at Hedeby are poorly furnished. This is partly

109 TOP LEFT *The Birka crucifix.* 110–11 BOTTOM LEFT AND TOP RIGHT *Eleventh-century silver crucifixes from Sweden, and* 112 CENTRE RIGHT AND BOTTOM RIGHT *from Trondheim, Norway.*

due to the fact that pagan graves of the Viking Age are generally less well equipped in Denmark than in Norway and Sweden. However, the Christian influences were felt more strongly there. From among the Christian objects found in the town, one might pick out what is in fact a perfectly ordinary disc brooch, but heavily gilt and ornamented with a strikingly simple representation of the Crucifixion.

The first Christian king of Norway was Håkon 'the Good', who died in 960. He had been brought up in England and became a popular and successful ruler, except in his attempts to convert his people. He met with such resistance that he himself relapsed into paganism before his death. The conversion of Norway was finally achieved by the two Olafs, Olaf Tryggvason (995–1000), and Olaf Haraldsson (1014–30), and by force rather than gentle persuasion. Olaf Tryggvason came to the throne a Christian and during his short reign is credited with the conversions of Norway, Orkney, the Faeroes, Iceland and Greenland. Such a conversion as that of Norway, enforced at sword-point, is unlikely to be effective in the long term, and it fell to Olaf Haraldsson to complete the task. It was probably during his reign that were made the fine pair of filigree ornamented crucifixes found in Trondheim (112). He was killed in battle at Stiklestad in 1030. Such had been his Christian zeal during his life, and such were the miracles arising from his death, that within a year his relics were enshrined and he was canonised – the first of the Scandinavian patron saints. It is probably his figure that we can recognise in quite another Christian context: the man with the forked beard, holding an axe, in the row on the front of the Irish reliquary of St Manchan, set among its elaborate Urnes-style decoration (107).

Serious missionary activity in Iceland got under way in the 980s with the work of Thorvald 'the Far-Travelled', although there had been Christians among the early settlers who had been converted in the British Isles. No lasting results were achieved, however, until the reign of Olaf Tryggvason, who first sent a priest of his own to the Icelanders and later threatened reprisals when progress was slow. Iceland came near to civil war on the issue, but a compromise was found to preserve legal order and peace. The conversion of the country was legally enacted at the General Assembly (Althing) of Iceland in 999, but certain freedoms for pagans were guaranteed. All Icelanders who were not already Christians had to be baptised, but sacrifice in secret was still permitted and no change was made in the customs of exposing newborn children (leaving them to die in the open air) and of eating horse-meat. At first headway was probably still slow, but within a few years the liberties that had been allowed to die-hard pagans were abolished.

Further progress for Christianity in Iceland was achieved by a number of missionary bishops who arrived to preach and teach, preparing men for the priesthood and consecrating churches. The first native bishop was Ísleif, son of one of the most important leaders in the Conversion: he was consecrated in 1056, by Bishop Adalbert of Bremen. Ísleif's see was based on the family estate at Skálholt, which was later given by his son Gizur, also his episcopal successor (1082–1118), to be the seat of Iceland's bishop in perpetuity. To the period of Ísleif or Gizur belongs the elegant bronze staff-head found by chance at Thingvellir (113). The crooks of this T-shaped object (or tau-cross) end in typical Urnes-style animal-heads. It is unique in the north, but will have adorned the staff of an ecclesiastic, although not necessarily that of a bishop.

The earliest church in Greenland was built on Eirík 'the Red's' farm at Brattahlíd at the beginning of the eleventh century by his wife Thjódhild. The story is that Eirík's son, Leif, was converted on a visit to Olaf Tryggvason in Norway, whence he returned with assistants to proclaim the new religion. The saga has it that 'his father Eirík was slow to become a convert, but his wife Thjódhild was soon persuaded, and she had a church

113 *Eleventh-century bronze staff-head (tau-cross) from Iceland.*

built at some distance from the houses. There she and the others who had accepted Christianity said their prayers. From the time Thjódhild adopted the faith, she refused to have intercourse with Eirík, and this he disliked very much . . .' A discarded soapstone weight on which is incised a crude Thor's hammer bears witness to the paganism of those first settlers at Brattahlíd.

Thjódhild's church was a tiny chapel with curved walls built of turf, for building timber was a rare commodity in Greenland. In Iceland and Scandinavia the earliest churches were of timber. The first stone churches cannot be seen as direct products of Viking civilisation. Although the stone cathedral at Lund was started in about 1080, it is an expression of the European tradition of Romanesque architecture. As such, both it and the other stone churches of Scandinavia fall outside the scope of this book. On the other hand, the wooden churches belong to the native architectural tradition and have a particular character of their own.

The first missionaries, like Ansgar at Hedeby and Birka, were concerned to get churches built even if they had to do it themselves. Then the first generations of Christians in Scandinavia built small churches for household use on their family estates. Despite the fact that these must have existed in large numbers – Adam of Bremen mentions that there were three hundred churches in the province of Skåne when King Sven (1047–74) established a bishop in Lund to administer them – only a handful of excavated examples are known, together with some fragments surviving because they were incorporated into later buildings.

The Flatatunga panels (114) have survived because they were reused as boarding in a succession of farmhouses in northern Iceland. In 1897 it was arranged that they should be removed and transferred to the museum, but before this could happen the five best panels, which formed part of the roof of the pantry, were destroyed by fire. Now only four panels remain, rescued from the roof of the living-room, but all in excellent condition despite their chequered history.

Their foliate ornament, in classic Ringerike style, has already been commented on, suggesting a date about the middle of the eleventh century. Below this ornament is a row of saints and so it seems unlikely that they were originally made to decorate a Viking hall. If the Flatatunga panels were carved for a small household church (and Flatatunga might be expected to have had one, being among the biggest farms in Iceland), then they are the earliest examples of church decoration surviving from the Scandinavian world.

The ornament of the Urnes Church portal in western Norway (115), which survived because it was incorporated into its twelfth-century successor, was described above. The first church at Urnes has been excavated and found to be a standard example of a group of eleventh-century 'stave-churches' known in Denmark, Sweden, Norway, and even England (at Greensted in Essex). Stave-construction means that the walls are made of upright planks, as seen in secular contexts earlier in the Viking Age at, for instance, Hedeby and Fyrkat. These churches have a rectangular nave and an approximately square chancel. Two have been excavated in Lund of which one, dating from about 1060, may have been the original cathedral. The church built by Harald at Jelling was also of this type; placed between the two great mounds, its traces lie beneath its stone replacement (69).

The principal reason that none of these churches survive is that in each case the planks were set directly in the ground and so in time rotted away (perhaps to be trimmed for reuse, as at Urnes and Greensted). All later stave-churches have their wall-planks set in sills laid on the ground, or on drystone foundations, as with the twelfth-century church at Urnes.

The appearance of these eleventh-century stave-churches can only be guessed at. But the first church at Urnes had four large posts set within the nave which may have served to heighten its roof, in the manner of later Norwegian churches. One like that at Borgund, also in the Sogn district of western Norway, with its multiple roofs and animal-headed gables, is a direct descendant of the first stave-churches built by the newly converted

114 *Incised wooden panels from Iceland, with Ringerike-style foliage patterns above a row of saints.*

115 *The twelfth-century stave-church at Urnes in western Norway incorporates part of an elegantly ornamented earlier building.*

landowners of the area. It may well demonstrate something of their superstructures, but at the same time it must be remembered that Borgund dates from the later twelfth century and is a far more elaborate building than the first church at Urnes ever was.

The theme of the Conversion of the North has taken us well beyond the end of the Viking Age. But then there is no particular moment at which the period can be said to have ended. It fades away. Settlers in England and in Ireland, in Normandy and in Russia, had gradually been absorbed into the native cultures of those areas. The Norman conquest of England in 1066 cannot remotely be described as a Viking invasion of a Scandinavian state. The Anglo-Saxons had previously regained control of their own lands, only to succumb to the Norman French. The invasion of England by Harald 'the Ruthless' had failed with his death earlier in 1066 at Stamford Bridge, and the invasion planned by St Knut of Denmark in 1085 proved abortive. Such events brought England's Viking Age to a close.

Elsewhere outside Scandinavia there were settlers still developing their Norse heritage. Orkney and Shetland remained Norwegian until 1468–9. Iceland remained an independent state until 1262–4, when the Norwegian King Håkon Håkonsson took control. The rise of the Norse settlements in Greenland was only beginning as the Viking Age was drawing to an end. At the same time developments within Scandinavia meant that, by the end of the eleventh century, the homelands from which most of these settlers had once set out had undergone significant changes.

Scandinavia had been drawn into a new cultural sphere – that of the European Christian community – with all the changes which that had entailed for the spiritual and legal basis of society. At the same time the trend had been towards centralised authority and the sole rule of kings. It was the Viking Age that saw the birth of the Christian nation-states of Scandinavia, that deeply influenced the history of the British Isles, that peopled the Faeroes and Iceland, and that, by chain of settlement, first brought America into direct contact (however briefly) with northern Europe.

From the Greenland Sea to the Caspian was a wide stage across which strode many remarkable figures during the Viking Age. Much of what they achieved depended on the skills, courage and endurance of ordinary men and women whose activities and experiences can now only be chronicled by archaeology, but every year brings new discoveries to shape and adjust our knowledge and appreciation of the many outstanding achievements of the Viking Age.

Select Bibliography

The following are some of the more important books in English.

Different treatments of the Viking theme can be found in:

B. Almgren (ed.), *The Viking* (C. A. Watts, 1966)
H. Arbman, *The Vikings* (Thames & Hudson, 1962)
J. Brøndsted, *The Vikings* (Penguin, 1965)
O. Klindt-Jensen and S. Ehren, *The World of the Vikings* (George Allen & Unwin, 1970)
D. M. Wilson, *The Vikings and Their Origins* (Thames & Hudson, 1970)

More exhaustive accounts with extensive bibliographies and guides to more specialised literature:

P. G. Foote and D. M. Wilson, *The Viking Achievement* (Sidgwick & Jackson, 1970)
G. Jones, *The History of the Vikings* (Oxford University Press, 1968)
P. H. Sawyer, *The Age of the Vikings* (Edward Arnold, 1977)

Some more specific topics are covered in:

M. Dolley, *Viking Coins of the Danelaw and of Dublin* (British Museum, 1965)
S. Jansson, *The Runes of Sweden* (Phoenix, 1962)
G. Jones, *The Norse Atlantic Saga* (Oxford University Press, 1964)
D. M. Wilson and O. Klindt-Jensen, *Viking Art* (George Allen & Unwin, 1966)
H. R. Loyn, *The Vikings in Britain* (Batsford, 1978)
E. Roesdahl, *Viking-Age Denmark* (British Museum Publications Ltd; provisional title, due for publication 1980).

A selection of modern translations of the Icelandic Sagas can be found in the Penguin Classics series.

For Children:

A. Civardi and J. A. Graham-Campbell, *The Time Traveller Book of Viking Raiders* (Usborne, 1977)
S. Hadenius and B. Janrup, *How They Lived in a Viking Settlement* (Lutterworth, 1976)

A complete and exhaustive description of all the items figured in this book is to be found in:

J. A. Graham-Campbell, *Viking Artefacts: A Select Catalogue* (British Museum Publications Ltd., 1980)

Index

List of Exhibits

The exhibition number is followed by an identification of the object, its materials, findspot and country, principal dimensions, museum and registration number (where available).

Abbreviations
The full title of museums or loaning institutions can be found by reference to the complete list of lenders on page 9. The following abbreviations have been made in this list:

Museums or loaning institutions:

Ber	Bergen University Historical Museum
BM MLA	British Museum, Department of Medieval and Later Antiquities
BM CM	British Museum, Department of Coins and Medals
Cop I	National Museum of Denmark, First Department
Cop II	National Museum of Denmark, Second Department
Dub	National Museum of Ireland
Ed	National Museum of Antiquities of Scotland
Hel	National Board of Antiquities, Helsinki
Hobro	Sydhimmerlands Museum
KMK	Royal Coin Cabinet, Stockholm
Kult	Culture History Museum, Lund
LUHM	Lund University Historical Museum
Oslo	University Museum of National Antiquities
OUMK	Oslo University Collection of Coins and Medals
Reyk	National Museum of Iceland
Ribe	Antiquities Museum
Roskilde	Viking Ship Museum
Rudkøbing	Langeland Museum
Sch	Schleswig Holstein Landesmuseum
SHM	National Antiquities Museum, Stockholm
Trond	Trondheim Royal Norwegian Scientific Society Museum
Uppsala	Museum for Nordic Antiquities
YAT	York Archaeological Trust (by courtesy of York District Council)
York	Yorkshire Museum

Findspots and countries:

Birka BE	Birka Black Earth (settlement area)
Den	Denmark
Eng	England
Fin	Finland
Ger	Germany
Ice	Iceland
Ire	Ireland
Nor	Norway
Sco	Scotland
Swe	Sweden

SECTION 1
Ships and the Sea

1 **Weather-vane**, gilt-bronze. Heggen (Nor).
L 27·8 cm. Oslo C23605.

2 **Anchor**, iron. Ribe (Den).
L 1·50 m. Ribe D 7887.

3 **Ship's rivets**, iron. Paviken (Swe).

4 **Clawed chisel**, iron. Paviken (Swe).
L 15·8 cm.

5 **Ship's stem-piece**, wood. Skuldelev wreck III (Den).
L 3·70 m. Roskilde.

6 **Ship's steering oar**, wood. Vorså (Den).
L 2·8 m. Frederikshavn.

7 **Ship's pail**, wood. Dublin (Ire).
H 30·5 cm. Dub E71:11220.

8 **Incised whetstone**. Löddeköpinge (Swe).
L 10·6 cm. LUHM.

9 **Plaque with ship incised**, slate. Jarlshof (Sco).
L 18 cm. Ed HSA 790.

10 **Boat model**, wood. Hedeby (Ger).
L 30 cm. Sch, old find.

11 **Boat model**, wood. Dublin (Ire).
L 11 cm. Dub E81:4228.

12 **Mould with dragon's head**, slate, with modern cast. Birka (Swe).
L 8·4 cm. SHM 8139:7.

13 **Fitting**, bronze. Saltvik Rangsby (Fin).
L 5·3 cm. Hel 4284:13.

14 **Picture-stone**. Smiss I (Swe).
H 1·26 m. SHM 11521.

15 **Ingot mould**, stone. Whitby (Eng).
L 26 cm. Whitby Abbey.

16 **Grave marker**, stone. Lindisfarne (Eng).
W 42 cm. Lindisfarne Museum.

17 **Hoard selection**, silver. Cuerdale (Eng). BM MLA 41, 7–11, 741.

SECTION 2
The Hedeby House

SECTION 3
House and Home

18 **Bowl**, bronze. Thumby-Bienebek grave 51 (Ger).
W 26 cm. Sch.

19 **Box and lid**, bronze. Findarve (Swe).
D 17·8 cm. SHM 1076.

20 **Ladle**, bronze. Birka grave 632 (Swe).
L 26·5 cm. SHM.

21 **Double bowl**, soapstone. Søndre Vik (Nor).
L 8·4 cm. Ber 8555p.

22 **Rectangular bowl**, soapstone. Finstad (Nor).
L 36 cm. Oslo C11317.

23 **Handled bowl**, soapstone. Lyngdal (Nor).
L 42·5 cm. Oslo C5718.

24 **Bowl**, soapstone. Kollsøyo (Nor).
D 57·5 cm. Ber 11495.

25 **Bowl**, pottery. Birka grave 731 (Swe).
D 17·7 cm. SHM.

26 **Pot**, clay. Birka grave 739 (Swe).
D 10 cm. SHM.

27 **Pot**, clay. Hedeby (Ger).
D 12 cm. Sch 11978:7.

28 **Pot**, clay. Lund (Swe).
D 18·5 cm. Kult 53436:522.

29 **Pot**, clay. Lund (Swe).
D 13·6 cm. Kult 53436:848.

30 **Horn mount**, silver on modern horn. Birka grave 523 (Swe).
D 7·5 cm. SHM.

31 **Pail**, wood. Lund (Swe).
D 34·5 cm. Kult 53436:839.

32 **Cup**, wood. Lund (Swe).
L 15 cm. Kult 66166:2997.

33 **Trencher**, wood. Hedeby (Ger).
L 32 cm. Sch Hb.63S6.3ϕ92.50+1.39.

34 **Bowl and spoon**, wood. Lund (Swe).
L 19·5 cm. Kult 53436:1093 and 793.

35 **Knife with handle**, iron and wood. Lund (Swe).
L 15·8 cm. Kult 53436:448.

36 **Drainaway**, wood. Lund (Swe).
L 48·5 cm. Kult 53436:1081.

37 **Strike-a-light**, iron. Marstein (Nor).
L 7·7 cm. Oslo C3463.

38 **Lamp**, iron. Hennum (Nor).
H 48 cm. Oslo C4626.

39 **Lamp**, soapstone. Jarlshof (Sco).
L 12·8 cm. Ed HSA 754.

40 **Lamp**, clay. Hedeby (Ger).
D 14 cm. Sch 11474:12.

41 **Cauldron and chain**, iron. Bengtsarvet (Swe).
H 99 cm. SHM 22293.

42 **Frying pan**, iron. Lekve (Nor).
L 66·5 cm. Ber 5490.

43 **Spit**, iron. Lund (Swe).
L 111 cm. Kult 66166:2007.

44 **Meat-fork**, iron. Sårheim (Nor).
L 13·5 cm. Ber 6735z.

45 **Shears**, iron. Ås (Nor).
L 19·7 cm. Oslo C5292g.

46 **Wool-comb**, iron. Tcrum (Nor).
L *c*. 9 cm. Ber 8991e.

47 **Spindle and whorl**, wood and clay. Ribe (Den).
Spindle L 29·7 cm. Ribe D 5781 and D 3791.

48 **Spindle whorl**, antler. Birka BE (Swe).
D 4·4 cm. SHM 5208:1819.

49 **Spindle**, wood. Hedeby (Ger).
L 17·6 cm.
Sch Hb.67N29.40ϕ210.60IX.

50 **Three loom weights**, clay. Hedeby (Ger).
Max. D 11·5 cm.
Sch Hb.63S13.15ϕ72+1.71 and Hb.68N7.85ϕ162.65V and Hb.66–69, stray find.

51 **Weaving comb**, antler. Birka BE (Swe).
L 12·1 cm. SHM 5208:910.

52 **Weaving batten**, whalebone. Ytre Elgsnes (Nor).
L 80·8 cm. Tromsø 3096c.

53 **Pin beater**, wood. Hedeby (Ger).
L 10 cm.
Sch Hb.69N10.2Dϕ217.30XIII.

54 **Pin beater**, bone. Birka BE (Swe).
L 15·4 cm. SHM 5208:1081.

55 **Two needles**, wood and bone. Hedeby (Ger).
Max. L 8·8 cm.
Sch Hb.62N50–54ϕc64–0.60–0.65 and Hb.69N27.10ϕ106.10VIII.

56 **Needle-case**, bone. Birka BE (Swe).
L 6·1 cm. SHM 5208:1532.

57 **Weaving tablet**, antler. Birka BE (Swe).
L 4·3 cm. SHM 5208:1644.

58 **Thread-maker**, bone. Lund (Swe).
L 5·8 cm. Kult 53436:572.

59 **Two pieces of woollen cloth**. Lund
60 (Swe).
L 3·9 cm. Kult 66166:989.

61 **Linen smoother**, glass. Hedeby (Ger).
D 7·8 cm. Sch Hb.37N5.15ϕ98.55–1.05.

62 **Linen**. Hedeby (Ger).
L 25 cm. Sch Hb.63 (Gewebe 1).

63 **Plaque**, whalebone. Loppasanden (Nor).
L 36 cm. Tromsø 6360h.

64 **Pipe**, eagle bone. Hedeby (Ger).
L 21·3 cm. Sch Hb.38S125–140ϕ96.35–96.45–1.65–1.70.

65 **Lyre bridge**, antler. Birka BE (Swe).
L 4·8 cm. SHM 5208:1634.

66 **Gaming-board**, wood. Ballinderry (Ire).
Max. L 36·2 cm. Dub 1932:6533.

67 **Dice**, bone. Nes (Nor).
L 3·2 cm. Ber 5161g.

68 **Playing-piece**, bone. Baldursheimur (Ice).
H 3·9 cm. Reyk 6.

69 **Two playing-pieces**, amber. Hedeby (Ger).
Max. D 2·2 cm.
Sch Hb.67N29.0ϕ198.50 and Hb.68N7.75ϕ174.10IV.

70 **Playing-pieces**, bone and gilt-bronze. Birka grave 624 (Swe). Max. H 3 cm. SHM.

71 **Twenty-three playing-pieces**, glass. Valsgärde grave 3 (Swe). Max. D 2·6 cm. Uppsala 59(3).

SECTION 4
Death and the Pagan Gods

72 **Hog-back grave stone**. Brompton (Eng). L 147·3 cm. Durham Cathedral Library: 60.

73 **Replica casket**. Cammin (Ger). L 60 cm. SHM.

74 **Four slabs of a grave cist**, stone. Ardre (Swe). Max. L 82·5 cm. SHM 11118/I,II,V,VI.

75 **Memorial stone**. Lillbjärs (Swe). H 86 cm. SHM 13742.

76 **Churchyard cross**, stone. Middleton (Eng). H 106 cm. Middleton church, stone B.

77 **Churchyard cross fragment**, slate. Andreas (Isle of Man). H 35·5 cm. Manx Museum no. 128.

78 **Grave slab**, stone. York Minster grave 1 (Eng). L 183 cm. York Museum.

79 **Two grave end-stones**. York Minster
80 grave 2 (Eng). Max. H 36·8 and 54·6 cm. York Museum.

81 **Gravestone fragment**. York (Eng). H 22·3 cm. York 1977.7.2115.

82 **Female skull**, bone. Ballateare (Isle of Man). Manx Museum.

83 **Cremation urn**, clay. Darum (Den). H 15 cm. Ribe 7190d.

84 **Model animal paw**, clay. Finström Godby (Fin). L 5·3 cm. Hel 3986:31.

85 **Sword**, iron. Wallstena (Swe). L 35·5 cm. SHM 2776.

86 **Thorshammer pendant on chain**, silver. Bredsätra (Swe). L 41·5 cm. SHM 101.

87 **Thorshammer pendant**, silver. Goldsborough (Eng). L 2·19 cm. Private possession.

88 **Thorshammer pendant**, silver. Rømersdal (Den). L *c*. 5 cm. Cop 597.

89 **Weight fragment with Thorshammer incised**, soapstone. Brattahlid (Greenland). L 7·8 cm. Cop II D12213.606.

90 **Mould**, soapstone. Trendgaarden (Den). L 9·8 cm. Cop I C24451.

91 **Pendant**, silver. Foss (Ice). L 5 cm. Reyk 6077.

92 **Two pins**, bone. Jarlshof (Sco). Max. L 12·8 cm. Ed HAS 7 and HAS 124.

93 **Amulet miniatures on ring**, silver. Klinta (Swe). D 3 cm. SHM 129.

94 **Key pendant**, leather. Ribe (Den). L 5 cm. Ribe D 6772.

95 **Phallus model**, wood. Danevirke (Ger). L 23 cm. Sch.

96 **Pendant**, silver. Fölhagen (Swe). H 1·2 cm. SHM 3547.

97 **Pendant**, silver. Birka grave 968 (Swe). H 1·6 cm. SHM.

98 **Neckring**, silver. Botnhamn (Nor). D 17·4 cm. Tromsø 1649.

99 **Rune-incised stave**, wood. Hedeby (Ger). L 12·1 cm. Sch Hb.III.

100 **Rune-incised bone**. Lund (Swe). L 14·2 cm. Kult 66166:1541.

101 **Skull fragment with incised runes**, bone. Ribe (Den). L 8·6 cm. Ribe D 13764.

102 **Penny of Sven Estridsson of Denmark**, silver. BM CM 1956, 4–8–71.

103 **Furnace stone**, soapstone. Snaptun (Den). W 24 cm. Århus 72a.

104 **Pendant**, silver. Aska (Swe). L 3·4 cm. SHM 16560.

105 **Two pendants**, silver. Fölhagen (Swe). Max. H 4·5 cm. SHM 3547.

106 **Man's head incised on stone fragment**. Jarlshof (Sco). L 11·5 cm. Ed HSA 793.

107 **Two foil sheets with male and female figures**, gold. Hauge (Nor). Max. L 0·9 cm. Ber 5392.

108 **Armed figure**, silver. Birka grave 571 (Swe). H 2·9 cm. SHM.

109 **Female figure**, silver. Klinta (Swe). H 2·8 cm. SHM 128.

110 **Female figure**, gilt-bronze. Öland (Swe). H 3 cm. SHM 6485.

111 **Male statuette**, bronze. Lindby (Swe). H 6·9 cm. SHM 13701.

112 **Playing-piece**, walrus ivory. Lund (Swe). H 4·7 cm. Kult 38252.

113 **Male figure**, bronze. Rällinge (Swe). H 6·9 cm. SHM 14232.

114 **Mount terminating in male head**, elk antler. Sigtuna (Swe). L 22 cm. SHM 22044.

SECTION 5
The Vikings

115 **Bow**, wood. Hedeby (Ger). L 1·92 m. Sch Hb.68.N14.00ϕ212.60X.

116 **Two arrow-heads**, iron. Estuna (Swe). Max. L 15·7 cm. SHM 27761.

117 **Arrow-nocks**, bronze. Hedeby (Ger). L 3·65 cm. Sch 12302.Bh.

118 **Spearhead**, iron. Birka grave 850 (Swe). L 55 cm. SHM.

119 **Spearhead**, iron. Fyrkat (Den). L 26·5 cm. Hobro D 1651–1966.

120 **Axe-head**, iron. Lund (Swe). L 14·2 cm. Kult 66166:1209.

121 **Axe-head**, iron. Thames (Eng). W 28 cm. BM MLA 38, 1–10,2.

122 **Axe-head**, iron. Fyrkat grave 2 no. 4 (Den). L 14·5 cm. Hobro D 150–1966.

123 **Mace head**, bronze. Norrkvie (Swe). L 7·1 cm. SHM 27778:1462.

124 **Spearhead**, iron, with silver and copper inlay. Kokemäki (Fin). L 33·5 cm. Hel 1174:8.

125 **Spearhead**, iron with copper and silver inlay. Thames (Eng). L 54·6 cm. BM MLA 93,7–15,2.

126 **Spearhead**, iron with silver inlay. Tingstäde (Swe). L 43·3 cm. SHM 7571:226.

127 **Spearhead**, iron with silver inlay. Valsgärde grave 12 (Swe). L 30·5 cm. Uppsala 59(12).

128 **Spearhead**, iron with silver inlay. Vesilahti (Fin). L 44·2 cm. Hel 439.

129 **Sword**, iron. Kjørven (Nor). L 91·6 cm. Oslo C19763.

130 **Sword hilt**, bronze. Eigg grave 1 (Sco). L 18·5 cm. Ed IL 157.

131 **Sword**, iron with copper and silver inlay. Barkarby (Swe). L 71 cm. SHM 19844:26.

132 **Sword**, gilt-silver and iron. Dybäck (Swe). L 52·3 cm. SHM 4515.

133 **Sword**, iron with silver and niello inlay. Hedeby (Ger). L 96·7 cm. Sch 12302.Bb.

134 **Sword**, iron with bronze inlay. Steinsvik (Nor). L 100·3 cm. Oslo C20317a.

135 **Sword**, bronze and iron. Tyrvänto Suontaka (Fin). L 91·5 cm. Hel 17.777:1.

136 **Scabbard chape (and part of blade)**, bronze and iron. Hafurbjarnarstadir (Ice). L 12·4 cm. Reyk 559.

137 **Scabbard chape**, bronze. Mänsälä (Fin).
L 7·7 cm. Hel 13941.

138 **Scabbard chape**, bronze. York (Eng).
L 8·6 cm. York 551.49.47.

139 **Shield boss**, iron. Haen (Nor).
D 14·5 cm. Oslo C14535.

140 **Shield boss**, iron. Hedeby (Ger).
D 16·3 cm. Sch 12302.Bc¹.

141 **Chain mail**, iron. Lund (Swe).
L 14 cm. Kult 66166:2917.

142 **Helmet**, iron. Gjermundbu (Nor).
H 23·7 cm. Oslo C27317k.

143 **Pair of spurs**, iron with silver inlay. Norre Longelse grave 2 (Den).
Max. L 21·3 cm. Rudkøbing C489.

144 **Stirrup**, iron with brass inlay. Thames at Battersea (Eng).
H 23·9 cm. BM MLA 54,4–24,1.

145 **Pair of stirrups**, iron with silver and copper inlay. Thumby-Bienebek grave I (Ger).
Max. H 22·8 cm. Sch.

The Viking Woman

146 **Female grave group**: Birka grave 854 (Swe). SHM.

Equal arm brooch, gilt-bronze.
L 17·6 cm.

Two mounts, gilt-silver.
Max. L 5·1 cm.

Two brooches, gilt-bronze and enamel.
Max. L 2·9 cm.

Two necklace spacers, gilt-silver.
Max. L 9·3 cm.

Beads, glass.
L 35 cm.

147 **Female grave group**: Ihre grave 414 (Swe). SHM 20826:370.

Box-shaped brooch, bronze.
D 5·4 cm.

Animal head brooches, bronze.
L 5·2 cm.

Eighteen mitre pendants, bronze.
L 3·6 cm.

Chains and suspension plates, bronze.
W 40 cm.

255 beads, calcite and glass.

Two spacers, bronze.
Max. L 6·9 cm.

Two pins, bronze.
Max. L 7·6 cm.

148 **Pair of oval brooches**, bronze. Norway.
Max. L 12·9 cm. Oslo C4727.

149 **Trefoil brooch**, bronze. Norway.
W 8·1 cm. Oslo C4730.

150 **Necklace**: twenty-seven mosaic beads. Eidem (Nor).
L 37 cm. Trond 8293.

151 **Female grave group**: Loppasanden (Nor). Tromsø 6360a,b,c,g.

Oval brooch pair, bronze.
L 10 cm.

Disc brooch, bronze.
D 6 cm.

Forty-five beads, glass and bronze.
L 62 cm.

152 **Disc brooch**, silver. Allmänninge (Swe).
D 9·3 cm. SHM 729:7.

153 **Disc brooch**, bronze. Dublin (Ire).
D 3·2 cm. L 7·1 cm. Dub E43:2086.

154 **Disc brooch**, bronze. Wisbech (Eng).
D 4·2 cm. Wisbech 1.1846.

155 **Disc brooch**, pewter. York (Eng).
D 3·6 cm. York 652.48.

156 **Disc brooch**, pewter. YAT (Eng).
D 3·1 cm. York 1977.7.1520.

157 **Disc brooch**, gold. Hedeby (Ger).
D 2·6 cm. Sch Hb.76, surface find.

158 **Box-shaped brooch**, gilt-bronze. Valla (Swe).
D 4·7 cm. SHM 5077.

159 **Tongue-shaped brooch**, bronze. Birka BE (Swe).
Max. L 10·2 cm. SHM 5208:147.

160 **Animal-head brooch**, bronze. Dalhem (Swe).
L 5·9 cm. SHM 1089.

161 **Oval brooch**, bronze. Kilmainham (Ire).
L 9·3 cm. Dub 1881:253.

162 **Oval brooch**, bronze. Hovindsholm (Nor).
L 9·4 cm. Oslo C172.

163 **Oval brooch**, bronze. Islay (Sco).
L 11·2 cm. Ed IL 215.

164 **Oval brooch**, gilt-bronze. Moscow region (USSR).
L 11·4 cm. SHM 18918.

165 **Oval brooch**, gilt-bronze and silver. Santon (Eng).
L 11·6 cm. BM MLA 88,1–3,1.

166 **Oval brooch**, gilt-bronze. Castletown (Sco).
L 11·1 cm. Ed IL 221.

167 **Oval brooch**, gilt-bronze. Nordland (Nor).
L 11·9 cm. Tromsø 2214.

168 **Equal-armed brooch**, silver. Birka grave 639 (Swe).
L 7·8 cm. SHM.

169 **Equal-armed brooch**, silver. Birka grave 973 (Swe).
L 7·9 cm. SHM.

170 **Animal-shaped brooch**, bronze. Kaupang (Nor).
L 7·9 cm. Oslo C27220n.

171 **Pair of toe rings**, silver. Fyrkat grave 4 (Den).
Max. D 1·5 cm. Hobro D170–1966.

172 **Armlet**, bronze. Birka grave 1081 (Swe).
D 7·3 cm. SHM.

173 **Strap fittings**, gilt-bronze. Lejre
174 (Den).
Max. L 4 cm. Cop I 1047–1050.

175 **Buckle-loop**, bronze. Barnes (Eng).
L 7·1 cm. BM MLA 56,7–1,1474.

176 **Strap-end**, bronze. York (Eng).
L 4·9 cm. York 1973.24.

177 **Strap-end**, gilt-silver. Winchester (Eng).
L 4 cm. Winchester CG.72.

178 **Strap-end**, bronze. Aggersborg (Den).
L 6·1 cm. Cop I A3–635.

179 **Toilet implements**, bronze. Hedeby (Ger).
Max. L 5·2 cm. Sch Hb. W131 and W145.

180 **Toilet implement**, gilt-silver and niello. Birka grave 507 (Swe).
L 6·9 cm. SHM.

181 **Knife-blade**, iron with bronze inlay. Lund (Swe).
L 9·7 cm. Kult 66166:2898.

182 **Knife**, iron, wood, silver. Fyrkat grave 22a (Den).
L 8·1 cm. Hobro D213–1966.

183 **Key pendant**, bronze. Hetland (Nor).
L 6·7 cm. Ber 1617.

184 **Key pendant**, bronze. Elstad (Nor).
L 9·8 cm. Oslo C3915.

185 **Two combs**, antler. Birka BE (Swe).
Max. L 18·5 cm. SHM 5208:751 and 564.

186 **Comb**, antler. Dublin (Ire).
L 15·5 cm. Dub E71:9785.

187 **Comb**, antler. Lund (Swe).
L 13·9 cm. Kult 66166:1511.

188 **Comb**, antler. Trondheim (Nor).
L 20 cm. Trond N39355.

189 **Comb and case**, antler. York (Eng).
L 14·1 cm. BM MLA 66,5–10,1.

190 **Ringed pin**, silver and niello. Birka grave 561 (Swe).
L 20·5 cm. SHM.

191 **Ball-headed pin**, bronze and gold. Birka grave 832 (Swe).
L 21·2 cm. SHM.

192 **Ball-headed pin**, silver. Thumby-Bienebek grave 21 (Ger).
L 13·1 cm. Sch.

193 **Ringed pin**, bronze. Birka grave 1007 (Swe).
L 18·8 cm. SHM.

194 **Ringed pin**, bronze. Dublin (Ire).
L 16·8 cm. Dub E43:1572.

195 **Ringed pin**, bronze. Gnúpverjaafréttur (Ice).
L 18·5 cm. Reyk 5396.

196 **Stick pin**, bronze. Dublin (Ire).
L 8·5 cm. Dub E43:551.

197 **Two pins**, bone. Jarlshof (Sco).
198 Max. L 11·3 cm. Ed HAS 3 and 4.

199 Pin, bone. Thames, London (Eng).
L 17 cm. BM MLA 93,6–18,72.

200 Pin, bone. Trondheim (Nor).
L 13·1 cm. Trond N37383.

201 Necklace, glass, silver, etc. Birka
grave 632 (Swe).
L 43 cm. SHM.

202 Necklace and disc brooch, glass and
gilt-bronze. Birka grave 948 (Swe).
L 90 cm. SHM.

203 Necklace, crystal, silver and glass.
Lilla Rone (Swe).
Max. H 3·3 cm. SHM 8315.

204 Collar of thirty-two pendants, gilt-
bronze, silver, gold. Krasse (Swe).
W 23 cm. SHM 6387.

205 Pendant, gold. Hedeby (Ger).
D 3·2 cm. Sch.

206 Pendant, gold. Ringome (Swe).
H 7·4 cm. SHM 4079.

207 Pendant, gilt-silver. Saffron Walden
(Eng).
H 5·5 cm. Saffron Walden Museum
1902.2.

SECTION 6
Viking Treasure

208 Carolingian coin pendant, silver.
Birka grave 66 (Swe). KMK.

209 Cufic coin pendant, silver. Birka
grave 731 (Swe). KMK.

210 Roman coin pendant, silver. Birka
grave 750 (Swe). SHM.

211 Carolingian coin pendant, silver.
Birka grave 978 (Swe). KMK.

212 Necklace of Anglo-Saxon coins,
silver. Äspinge (Swe).
L 40·4 cm. SHM 6620:20.

213 Necklace with coins and pendants,
silver. Hämeenlinna (Fin).
L 50 cm. Hel 3090:1.

214 Disc brooch, silver. Garsnäs (Swe).
D 5·4 cm. LUHM 6609.

215 Penannular brooch, silver and gold.
Hatteberg (Nor).
L 21 cm. Ber 8377c.

216 Thistle brooch, silver. Laitila (Fin).
L 36·7 cm. Hel 11243.

217 Penannular brooch, silver and gold.
Møllerløkken (Den).
L 31·2 cm Cop I 16370.

218 Thistle brooch, silver. Newbiggin
(Eng).
L 51·2 cm. BM MLA 1909,6–24,2.

219 Penannular brooch, silver. Skaill
(Sco).
L 38 cm. Ed IL 1.

220 Penannular brooch, silver. Vible
(Swe).
L 7·3 cm. SHM 108.

221 Neckring, gold. Tissø (Den).
D c. 35 cm. Cop I Dnf 1/77.

222 Box-shaped brooch, gold, silver,
niello and bronze. Mårtens (Swe).
D 7·5 cm. SHM 12151:9.

223 Disc brooch, gold. Hedeby (Ger).
D 3·9 cm. Sch KS 10596.

224 Two disc brooches, gold. Hornelund
(Den).
Max. D 8·6 cm. Cop I C7144 and 5.

225 Two neckrings, silver. Ytlings (Swe).
Max. D 13·4 cm. SHM 8489.

226 Armlet, silver. Bryungs (Swe).
D 9 cm. SHM 15903.

227 Armring, silver. Skaill (Sco).
D 11 cm. Ed IL 22.

228 Armring, gold. Oxna (Sco).
D 7·5 cm. Ed FE 71.

229 Armring, gold. Virginia (Ire).
D 7·2 cm. BM MLA 49,3–1,2.

230 Finger ring, gold. Simrishamn (Swe).
D 3·3 cm. SHM 7065.

231 Finger ring, gold. Tundergarth (Sco).
D 2·6 cm. BM MLA AF 466.

232 Hoard and dish, silver and iron.
Birka BE (Swe).
Dish D 23·5 cm. SHM 5208:3.

233 Armlet hoard, silver. Mårtens (Swe).
D 9·3 cm. SHM 12151 1–8.

234 Hoard of armrings and neckrings,
silver. Sandby (Swe).
Max. D 18 cm. SHM 936.

235 Neckrings, silver. Skaill (Sco).
Max. D 17·5 cm. Ed IL 18 and 20.

236 Two armrings and a finger ring,
silver. Fyrkat (Den).
Max. D 10·5 cm. Hobro D57 and
D381–1966.

237 Finger ring hoard, gold. Stenness
(Sco).
D 2·8 cm. Ed FE 27–30.

238 Armring, gold. Goodrington (Eng).
D 9 cm. BM MLA 1979,10–1,1.

239 Two armrings, gold. Dublin (Ire).
D 9·8 cm. Dub E71:9007 and 8.

240 Armring, gold. Ornum (Den).
D 8·3 cm. Cop I C5509.

241 Armring, gold. Hornelund (Den).
D 7·1 cm. Cop I C7146.

242 Armring, gold. Wipholm (Ger).
D 9 cm. Sch LMS KS.6421.

243 Armring, silver. Brahesminde (Den).
D 8·6 cm. Cop I Dnf 14/48.

244 Two armrings, silver. Ireland.
Max. D 6·9 cm. Dub W62 and W63.

245 Armring, silver. Ivö (Swe).
D 9·1 cm. SHM 2406.

246 Disc brooch, silver. Sutton (Eng).
D 16·4 cm. BM MLA 1951,10–1,1.

247 Cup, silver and gilt. Lejre (Den).
D 5·9 cm. Cop I 11373.

SECTION 7
Trade and Loot

248 Selection of grave goods. Paksujoki,
Zaljuščik, Mound 1 (USSR).

Male grave B

Horse-bit, iron.
L 21 cm. Hel 1675:17.

Sword, iron inlaid with silver and
copper.
L 96·5 cm. Hel 1675:1.

Spearhead, iron.
L 46·8 cm. Hel 1675:2.

Spearhead, iron.
L 27·8 cm. Hel 1675:3.

Axe-head, iron.
L 15·5 cm. Hel 1675:7.

Female grave B1

Oval brooches, bronze and iron.
Max. L 11 cm. 1675:22 and 23.

Disc brooch, bronze.
D 16·9 cm. Hel 1675:21.

Chains, bronze.
Ring D 1 cm. Hel 1675:32.

Pendant, bronze.
L 12·5 cm. Hel 1675:25.

Beads, carnelian, glass, silver and gold
foil. Hel 1675:30.

Armring, silver.
D 6 cm. Hel 1675:27.

249 Cremation urn, clay. Paksujoki,
Zaljuščik, Mound 1 (USSR).
D 16 cm. Hel 10157:1, 8.

250 Scales, weights and bag, tinned-
bronze, lead and linen. Jåtten (Nor).
Max. L 18·5 cm. Ber 4772.

251 Scales box, bronze. Petes (Swe).
D 8·7 cm. SHM 792.

252 Weights, lead, gilt-bronze, amber and
enamel. Kiloran Bay (Sco).
Max. L 3·3 cm. Ed L 1924,12–18.

253 Weights, lead, gilt-bronze, silver,
enamel and glass. Kilmainham (Ire).
Max. D 3·7 cm.
Dub 2389,2399–401,2413–7.

254 Two ingots, silver. Cuerdale (Eng).
BM MLA 41,7–11,10 and 103.

255 Ingot mould, soapstone. Hedeby
(Ger).
L 11·9 cm.
Sch Hb.34So.60ø87.80,0.70.

256 Group of hacksilver. Cuerdale
(Eng). BM MLA
41,7–11,141,142,518,677.

257 Armring, silver. Skaill (Sco).
Max. D 7·7 cm. Ed IL 30 and 31.

258 Counterfeit armlet, bronze and tin.
Tystebols (Swe).
L 13·2 cm. SHM 16835.

259 Cufic coin fragments. Cuerdale
(Eng). BM CM 41,7–10,1442 and
1444.

260 Cufic coin hoard, silver. Fittja (Swe). KMK.

261 Bucket, bronze and wood. Birka grave 507 (Swe). H 18·5 cm. SHM.

262 Reliquary, wood, bronze, tinned copper, glass or garnet. Norway. L 13·6 cm. Cop II 9084.

263 Terminal, bronze, glass, and enamel. Helgö (Swe). H 9·3 cm. SHM 25075:1000.

264 Stud, glass. Hedeby (Ger). D 2·6 cm. Sch 13710.

265 Mount, gilt-bronze, amber and glass. Romfø (Nor). L 8·9 cm. Oslo C6185.

266 Ringed pin, gilt-silver, gold, amber and glass. Westness (Sco). L 17·4 cm. Ed IL 728.

267 Disc brooch, gilt-bronze. Sommarøy (Nor). D 8·8 cm. Tromsø 4052b.

268 Mount, gilt-bronze. Bjørke (Nor). L 9·7 cm. Ber 8256.

269 Hooked tag, silver. Birka grave 348 (Swe). L 3·1 cm. SHM.

270 Anglo-Saxon silver pennies found in Sweden. KMK.

Edward the Elder (899–924).

Aethelred II, struck 991–7, London.

Knut 'the Great', struck c. 1018–24, Oxford.

Harold I, struck 1036–7, Bristol.

Edward the Confessor, struck 1044–6, London.

271 Tating-ware jug, pottery with tin appliqués. Birka grave 854 (Swe). H 24·7 cm. SHM.

272 Funnel beaker, glass. Birka grave 577 (Swe). H 15·3 cm. SHM.

273 Beaker, glass. Birka grave 539 (Swe). H 13·5 cm. SHM.

274 Trefoil mount, gilt-silver. Huseby (Nor). W 6·6 cm. Trond 8526.

275 Belt mounts, gilt-silver. Ö.Påboda (Swe). Max. L 13·6 cm. SHM 1296.

276 Cup, silver-gilt. Fejø (Den). D 11·4 cm. Cop I C1458.

277 Quern, lavastone. Hedeby (Ger). L 27·5 cm. Sch Hb.67N24.35ø210.10VI.

278 Selection of imported glass (sherds). Kaupang (Nor). Oslo.

279 Selection of imported pottery (sherds). Kaupang (Nor). Oslo.

280 Sword-blade fragment with maker's mark, iron. Sääksmaki (Fin). L 22 cm. Hel 2767.

281 German silver coins. Sweden. SHM 18744.

Otto I or II penny, struck 965–83, Cologne.

Henry II penny, struck 985–95, Regensburg.

Otto III penny, struck 983–96, Huy.

282 Pot, clay. Trelleborg (Den). D 19 cm. Cop II Q253.

283 Necklace, silver. Fölhagen (Swe). L 61·5 cm. SHM 3547.

284 Earring, silver. Runsberga (Swe). H 8·7 cm. SHM 12080.

285 Earring, silver. Sturkø (Swe). H 5·6 cm. SHM 8770.

286 Pendant, silver. Sweden. W 4·6 cm. SHM (unregistered).

287 Pendant on chain, silver. Eidet Indre (Nor). Pendant H 11·5 cm. Tromsø 4400a.

288 Strike-a-light, bronze and iron. Åse (Nor). L 7 cm. Ber 4336b.

289 Reliquary on chain, silver. Allmäninge (Swe). L 26 cm. SHM 729:1.

290 Pendant cross, silver. Norsborg (Swe). L 5·6 cm. SHM 21555.

291 Egg, glazed clay. Sigtuna (Swe). H 4·4 cm. SHM 18562.

292 Cap mount and four tassels, silver wire. Birka grave 581 (Swe). Max. L 6·6 cm. SHM.

293 Spindle whorl, slate. Lund (Swe). D 2·5 cm. Kult 53436:588.

294 Silver srebrennik of Jaroslav 'the Wise' of Kiev (1016–54). KMK.

295 Coin brooch, gold. Hedeby (Ger). D 2·3 cm. Sch Hb.39N71.65 W102.23–1,99.

296 Byzantine seal, lead. Hedeby (Ger). D 2·7 cm. Sch Hb.66N10.30ø96.98+1.73.

297 Taffeta, silk. Lund (Swe). L 13·5 cm. Kult KM 53436:517.

298 Cuffs and cloak-tie, gold-embroidered silk. Mammen (Den). Cop I C138 and C139.

299 Cuff, silver-embroidered silk. Valsgärde grave 12 (Swe). Uppsala.

300 Brazier, bronze. Åbyn (Swe). H 33 cm. Gävle 9699.

301 Flask with Arab inscription, bronze. Aska (Swe). H 32 cm. SHM 16560.

302 Bowl, silver. Alvkarleby (Swe). D 14·2 cm. SHM Med Dep 133.

303 Glazed cup, Hemse (Swe). D 6·2 cm. SHM 5035.

304 Caucasian silver dirham, found in the Cuerdale hoard (Eng). Max D 2·5 cm. BM CM 1841,7–10,1436.

305 Samanid silver dirham, struck 906–7. Goldsborough hoard (Eng). D 2·7 cm. BM CM.

306 Mounts and pendants, gilt-silver. Vårby (Swe). Max. L 5·8 cm. SHM 4516.

SECTION 8
The Craftsman

307 Pendant whetstone, slate. Birka grave 496 (Swe). L 13·3 cm. SHM.

308 Pendant whetstone, slate. Birka grave 605B (Swe). L 6·4 cm. SHM.

309 Pendant whetstone, slate. Birka grave 644 (Swe). L 8·5 cm. SHM.

310 Beads and worked fragments, carnelian. Hedeby (Ger). Sch.

311 Rock crystal, in various stages of working. Hedeby (Ger). Sch.

312 Playing-piece, jet. Bawdsey (Eng). H 4·7 cm. Ipswich 969–63.

313 Armring, jet. Castletown (Sco). D 6·8 cm. Ed FN 2.

314 Armring, jet. Høiland (Nor). D 5·3 cm. Ber 5628.

315 Gripping bears, jet. Tresfjorden (Nor). L 4·5 cm. Ber 290.

316 Snake pendant, jet. Longva (Nor). D 4·2 cm. Ber 9471b.

317 Snake pendant, jet. York (Eng). H 5·2 cm. York H.110.

318 Model cat, amber. Birka BE (Swe). L 3 cm. SHM 5208:8252.

319 Selection of worked amber and raw material. Hedeby (Ger). Sch Hb.38S68ø204.50,4–0,5.

320 Mosaic and other fragments, glass. Paviken (Swe).

321 Crucible, clay. Lincoln (Eng). D 7·7 cm. Lincoln F75. G72.P190.

322 Mosaic glass beads and manufacturing debris, glass. Ribe (Den). Ribe.

323 Selection of glass debris. Kaupang (Nor). Oslo.

324 Finger rings, glass. Lincoln (Eng). D 2·4 cm. Lincoln F75. G224, F75. G244 and F75. G205.

325 Comb working fragments, antler. Hedeby (Ger). Max. L 15·8 cm. Sch Hb.1935–38, and 1969, and Hb.69N26.50–27.50ø95.50–96.50III.

326 Comb, Hedeby (Ger).
L 20·9 cm.
Sch Hb.164S5.00φ83.00+1.02.

327 Rough-cut disc, antler. Hedeby (Ger).
D 5·2 cm. Sch.

328 Pin, bone. Hedeby (Ger).
L 14·4 cm. Sch Hb.69N30.60φ30.85IX.

329 Pin, bone. Lund (Swe).
L 11·5 cm. Kult 66166:853.

330 Spoon, antler. Birka BE (Swe).
L 14·4 cm. SHM 5208:550.

331 Handle, antler. Birka BE (Swe).
L 8·3 cm. SHM 5208:945.

332 Sword pommel and lower guard, antler. Birka BE (Swe).
Max. L 9·4 cm. SHM 5208:542 and 544.

333 Arrow-head, antler. Hedeby (Ger).
L 4·9 cm. Sch Hb.66N22.65φ16.70X.

334 Cleaver, whalebone. Tisnes (Nor).
L 12·1 cm. Tromsø 799.

335 Handle, antler. York (Eng).
L 8·5 cm. BM MLA 1942,10-7,2.

336 Plaque, whalebone. Grytøy (Nor).
H 34·5 cm. Ber 272.

337 Model duck, elkhorn. Birka BE (Swe).
L 13·2 cm. SHM 5208:1604.

338 Two playing-pieces, bone. Hedeby (Ger).
D 3·6 cm. Sch Hb.67N29.60φ200.90VI and Hb.67N13.00φ201.60III.

339 Carved plank, wood. Trondheim (Nor).
L 150 cm. Trond N30000.

340 Carved mount, wood. Dublin (Ire).
L 27·5 cm. Dub E172:4309

341 Bowl with sculpted handle, wood. Hedeby (Ger).
L 37 cm. Sch Hb.69N6.70φ63.50XII.

342 Box and lid, wood. Dublin (Ire).
L 15·5 cm. Dub E122:17155.

343 Spoon, wood. Hedeby (Ger).
L 12·5 cm. Sch Hb.1963/64.

344 Spoon, wood. Trondheim (Nor).
L 18·6 cm. Trond N36697.

345 Turned mug, wood. York (Eng).
D 11·6 cm. YAT 1977.7 1384.

346 Turned bowl, wood. York (Eng).
D 18 cm. YAT 1977.7 1383.

347 Core, wood. York (Eng).
D 6·6 cm. YAT 1977.7 2351.

348 Box, bark. Hedeby (Ger).
D 18·4 cm.
Sch Hb.64S5.80φ90.70+0.59.

349 Axe-blanks on wooden pole, iron. Gjerrild (Den).
L 73·5 cm. Cop I C24854.

350 Blank, iron. Alborga (Swe).
L 41 cm. SHM 1006.

351 Eight blanks, iron. Somdalen (Nor).
Max. L 30·2 cm. Oslo C2264-5.

352 Tool chest, iron and wood. Mästermyr (Swe).
L 90 cm. SHM 21592.

353– Thirty-two tools, iron, with modern
358 wood handles. Mästermyr (Swe).
Max. L 51 cm. SHM 21592.

359 Metalsmith's tools, iron, with modern wood handles. Bygland (Nor).
Max. L 62·1 cm. Oslo C27454.

360 Selections of whetstones. Kaupang (Nor). Oslo.

361 Norwegian whetstone. York (Eng).
L 17 cm. YAT 1972.21.5156.

362 Pattern-welded spearhead, iron. Valkjärvi (Fin).
L 45·5 cm. Hel 3870:2.

363 Shoe, leather. Lund (Swe).
L 21·5 cm. Kult 66166:1045.

364 Shoe, leather. Ribe (Den).
L 29·8 cm. Ribe D 6100.

365 Ankle-boot, leather. York (Eng).
L 23 cm. YAT 1974.8.11.

366 Knife, bone and iron. Canterbury (Eng).
L 10·6 cm. Canterbury.

367 Shoe-last, wood. Hedeby (Ger).
L 13·5 cm. Sch Hb.69N65W13.35XII.

368 Awl, iron and wood. York (Eng).
L 9·7 cm. YAT 1974.21 5403.

369 Scabbard, leather. York (Eng).
L 34 cm. YAT 1976.11 73.

370 Sherds selection, soapstone. Kaupang (Nor). Oslo.

371 Bowl, soapstone. Landvikvannet (Nor).
D 24 cm. Olso C21813e.

372 Ingot mould, soapstone. Kaupang (Nor).
L 12 cm. Oslo Div A 63g.

373 Weight, soapstone. Hedeby (Ger).
H 6·2 cm.
Sch Hb.64N19.50φ83.90+2.65.

374 Spindle whorl, soapstone. Jarlshof (Sco).
D 3·4 cm. Ed HSA 416.

375 Spindle whorl and unfinished whorl, soapstone. Brattahlíd (Greenland).
L 7·5 cm.
Cop II D12205.980 and 12204.742.

376 Trial-piece, slate. Killaloe (Ire).
L 9 cm. BM MLA 58,1-20,1.

377– Trial-pieces, bone and stone, found
382 in Dublin (Ire). Dub.

377 Incised with quatrefoils, bone.
L 14·5 cm. E122:9270.

378 Incised with quatrefoils, bone.
L 16 cm. E122:6543.

379 Borre style ring-chain, bone.
L 14·9 cm. E122:6567.

380 Borre style ring-chain, bone.
L 14·9 cm. E43:2327.

381 Ringerike style patterns, bone.
L 11·6 cm. E71:708.

382 Animal interlace patterns, stone.
L 11·4 cm. E122:8760.

SECTION 9
Kings, Coinage and Subsistence

383 Silver penny, Guthrum (Athelstan II) of East Anglia, struck c. 885. BM CM 1838,7-10,8.

384 Silver penny, St Edmund Memorial issue, struck c. 895. BM CM 1838,7-10-771.

385 Silver penny, Siefred, struck c. 896, York. BM CM 1838,7-10-1233.

386 Silver penny, Mirabilia fecit issue, struck c. 900, York. BM CM 1838,7-10-1410.

387 Silver penny, Cnut, struck c. 900, York. BM CM 1838,7-10-1295.

388 Silver halfpenny, Cnut, struck c. 900, York. BM CM 1838,7-10-1394.

389 Silver penny, Cnut, struck c. 900, York. BM CM 1838,7-10-1265.

390 Silver penny, Cnut, struck c. 900, Quentovic. BM CM 1838,7-10-1424.

391 Silver penny, St Peter of York, struck c. 910, York. BM CM 1915,5-7-772.

392 Silver penny, St Peter of York, struck c. 915, York. BM CM 1935,11-17-369.

393 Silver penny, St Peter of York, struck c. 918, York. BMC 1122.

394 Silver penny, St Martin of Lincoln, struck c. 915, Lincoln. BMC 698.

395 Silver penny, Raienalt, struck 919-21, York. BMC 1083.

396 Silver penny, Raienalt, struck 919-21, York. BM CM 1862,9-26-4.

397 Silver penny, Raienalt, struck 919-21, York. BMC 1087.

398 Silver penny, 'Edward', struck c. 920, York. BM CM 1959,12-10-2.

399 Silver penny, Anlaf Guthfrithsson, struck c. 940, York. BM CM 1862,9-30-1.

400 Silver penny, Anlaf Sihtricsson, struck c. 941-3, York. BM CM 1915,5-7-767.

401 Silver penny, Anlaf Sihtricsson, struck c. 941-3, York. BMC 1090.

402 Record-piece or coin-weight, lead, struck c. 943, York. BM CM 1876,8-4-2.

403 Silver penny, Eric 'Bloodaxe', struck 952-4, York. BMC 1112.

404 **Silver penny**, Hedeby group, struck *c.* 825, Hedeby. KMK.

405 **Silver penny**, Carolingian group, struck 975, Hedeby. KMK.

406 **Silver penny**, Harald 'Bluetooth', struck *c.* 975–*c.* 980, Jelling. BM CM 1925,2–4–30.

407 **Silver penny**, Olaf 'Skötkonung', struck *c.* 995–1000, Sigtuna. BM CM 1840,3–11–11.

408 **Silver penny**, imitation of Aethelred II, struck *c.* 1000–1018. KMK.

409 **Silver penny**, Olaf Haraldsson, struck *c.* 1017–25. KMK SNM 2185.

410 **Silver penny**, Harald 'the Ruthless', struck *c.* 1047–55. OUMK.

411 **Silver penny**, Harald 'the Ruthless', struck *c.* 1055–65. OUMK.

412 **Silver penny**, Olaf Haraldsson, struck *c.* 1019–28. OUMK FC 200.

413 **Silver penny**, Olaf 'the Quiet', struck 1067–80. OUMK.

414 **Silver penny**, Harald 'the Ruthless', struck *c.* 1055–65. OUMK FC 1159–60.

415 **Silver penny**, Olaf 'the Quiet', struck *c.* 1067–80. OUMK FC 1159–60.

416 **Silver penny**, Cnut, struck *c.* 1018, Lund. BM CM 1956,4–8–58.

417 **Silver penny**, Cnut, struck *c.* 1018–*c.* 1020, Lund. BM CM 1925,2–4–32.

418 **Silver penny**, Cnut, struck *c.* 1018–*c.* 1020. Viborg KMK.

419 **Silver penny**, Cnut, struck *c.* 1020–*c.* 1030, Lund. BM CM 1925,2–4–33.

420 **Silver penny**, Cnut, struck *c.* 1020–*c.* 1030, Orbaek. KMK.

421 **Silver penny**, Cnut, struck *c.* 1028, Sigtuna. KMK.

422 **Silver penny**, Cnut, struck *c.* 1018–24, Bath. BMC 5.

423 **Silver penny**, Cnut, struck *c.* 1024–30, Winchester. BMC 581.

424 **Silver penny**, Harthacnut (1035–42), Lund. BM CM 1956,4–8–69.

425 **Silver penny**, Harthacnut, struck 1035–7, London. BM CM 1935,11–17–614.

426 **Silver penny**, Sven Estridssen, struck *c.* 1044–7, Lund. BM CM 1906,11–3–5142.

427 **Silver penny**, Sven Estridssen, struck before *c.* 1065, Lund. BM CM 1956,4–8–87.

428 **Silver penny**, Sihtric III, struck *c.* 997, Dublin. BM CM 1838,9–19–9.

429 **Silver penny**, Anonymous issue, struck *c.* 1065, Dublin. BM CM 1957,6–12–36.

430 **Shovel**, wood. Danevirke (Ger). L 83·8 cm. Sch.

431 **Quern**, stone. Ribe (Den). D 43 cm. Ribe D 7877 and 8.

432 **Ploughshare**, iron. Furnes (Nor). L 20·8 cm. Oslo C169a.

433 **Farmer's tools from a hoard**, iron. Skårud (Nor). Max. L 44·8 cm. Oslo C3417–21.

434 **Sickle**, iron. Tranby (Nor). L 24·5 cm. Oslo C26927d.

435 **Leaf knife**, iron. Halstad (Nor). L 33·5 cm. Oslo C21098d.

436 **Bell**, bronze. Åsheim (Nor). H 6·8 cm. Oslo C25885c.

437 **Shears**, iron. Åker (Nor). L 32·3 cm. Oslo C4718.

438 **Two fish hooks**, iron. Lund (Swe). L 6·5 cm. Kult 53436:226.

439 **Line-winder**, whalebone. Sømhovd (Nor). L 20 cm. Trond 13471.

440 **Fish-gorge**, bone. Birka BE (Swe). L 4·5 cm. SHM 5208:964.

441 **Net-float**, bark. Lund (Swe). L 12·2 cm. Kult 53436:719.

442 **Weight**, stone. York (Eng). H 12·2 cm. York C658.

443 **Net-stick**, wood. Lund (Swe). L 24·8 cm. 53436:61.

444 **Fishing spear**, iron. Fossesholm (Nor). L 19·5 cm. Oslo C1272.

445 **Leister**, iron. Rise (Nor). L 30 cm. Trond 7319.

446 **Three arrow-heads**, wood. Hedeby (Ger). L 9·5 cm. Sch Hb.68N18.60φ229.60VII, Hb.68N39.50φ213.10VIII and Hb.67N24.55φ219.60VIII.

447 **Six arrow-heads**, iron. Estuna (Swe). Max. L 12·5 cm. SHM 27761.

448 **Two spearheads**, iron. Estuna (Swe). Max. L 25·7 cm. SHM 27761.

449 **Ski**, wood. Muolaa (Fin). L 194 cm. Hel KM 7406.

450 **Two skates**, bone. Lund (Swe). L 22 cm. Kult 66166:1044 and 2261.

451 **Crampon**, iron. Lund (Swe). W 4·6 cm. Kult 66166:764.

452 **Two crampons**, iron. Lund (Swe). Max. H 6·5 cm. Kult 53436:571 and 1131.

453 **Rattle and hooks**, iron. Nordgård (Nor). L 23 cm. Oslo C576–7.

454 **Horse harness bow**, gilt-bronze and modern wood. Elstrup (Den). L 48 cm. Sch.

455 **Horse harness mount**, gilt-bronze. Birka grave 750 (Swe). L 12·5 cm. SHM.

456 **Stirrup**, iron. Nordgård (Nor) W 13·1 cm. Oslo C575.

457 **Horse bit**, iron. By (Nor). L 28·3 cm. Oslo C10716.

SECTION 10
Art and Ornament

458 **Furnace stone**, soapstone. Hedeby (Ger). L 19·5 cm. Sch.

459 **Ingot**, bronze. Lund (Swe). L 7 cm. Kult 53436:614.

460 **Ingot**, bronze. Birka BE (Swe). L 17·5 cm. SHM 5208:2512.

461 **Crucible**, clay. Lund (Swe). H 4·0 cm. Kult 53436:199.

462 **Three crucibles**, clay. Hedeby (Ger). H 9·5 cm. Sch Hb.

463 **Crucible**, clay. Kaupang (Nor). H 4·8 cm. Oslo K1960 MO.

464 **Crucible**, clay. Birka BE (Swe). H 4·2 cm. SHM 5208:2484.

465 **Unfinished brooch and mould**, bronze and clay. Lund (Swe). H 2·8 cm. Kult 66166:2626 and 7.

467 **Oval brooch mould fragments**, clay. Ribe (Den). Ribe D 10469 and D 10442.

468 **Oval brooch**, gilt-bronze. Hjallese Torp (Den). L 9·5 cm. Cop I C23184.

469 **Scabbard chape mould fragment**, clay. Birka BE (Swe). H 4·6 cm. SHM 5208:2497.

470 **Scabbard chape**, bronze. Åstad (Swe). L 6·5 cm. SHM 17968.

471 **Mould for thistle brooch pin**, siltstone. Kaupang (Nor). L 8 cm. Oslo K1960. M.O. Br.Bl.s.a.

472 **Thistle brooch**, bronze. Marum (Nor). D 6·8 cm. Oslo C11285.

473 **Trefoil brooch mould**, clay. York (Eng). L 10·7 cm. YAT 1975.6 448.

474 **Trefoil brooch**, gilt-silver and gold. Mosnes (Nor). W 7·8 cm. Ber 4342.

475 **Pendant mould (and modern impression)**, sandstone. Hedeby (Ger). Sch.

476 **Pendant mould**, soapstone. Hedeby (Ger). L 5·3 cm. Sch KS D203.

477 **Ingot**, lead. Kaupang (Nor). L 8·7 cm. Oslo K1962–C.

478 **Trefoil brooch mould fragment,** clay. Hedeby (Ger).
L 5·4 cm. Sch 13710.

479 **Trefoil brooch,** pewter. Hedeby (Ger).
W 4·7 cm.
Sch Hb.34φ781.65S0.85,0.70.

480 **Disc brooch mould,** antler. Hedeby (Ger).
D 5·2 cm.
Sch Hb.64N15–20φ95–100II.

481 **Quatrefoil brooch mould,** antler. Hedeby (Ger).
L 8·3 cm.
Sch Hb.34S0.50φ158.50:0.20.

482 **Hammered ingot,** bronze. Lund (Swe).
L 18 cm. Kult 66166:770.

483 **Patrice for disc brooch (and modern impression),** bronze. Hedeby (Ger). Sch Hb.38, Bachbett, Sch 8.

484 **Stamping pad,** lead and iron punch. Mästermyr (Swe). Max. L 7·5 cm. SHM 21592.

485 **Armlet,** silver. Gotland (Swe).
D 7·3 cm. BM MLA 1921,11–1,305.

486 **Draw plate,** iron. Mästermyr (Swe).
L 13·7 cm. SHM 21592.

487 **Wire,** bronze. Tystebols (Swe).
D 5 cm. SHM 16835.

488 **Wire,** silver. Botvalde (Swe).
D 3·8 cm. SHM 23228.

489 **Knitted wire braiding,** silver. Inchkenneth (Sco).
L 46 cm. BM MLA 51,6–13,1

490 **Heating tray,** clay with silver granules. Fyrkat (Den).
D 7·1 cm. Hobro D1229A–1966.

491 **Hammer,** iron. Birka BE (Swe).
L 10·9 cm. SHM 5208:438.

492 **Hammer head,** antler. Birka BE (Swe).
L 10 cm. SHM 5208:928.

493 **Vice,** antler. Hedeby (Ger).
L 9·8 cm. Sch.

494 **Annular brooch,** gilt-bronze, gold, silver and niello. Austris (Swe).
L 10·5 cm. SHM 8211.

495 **Nine bridle mounts,** gilt-bronze. Broa (Swe).
Max. L 9·0 cm. SHM 10796.

496 **Oval brooch,** bronze. Asen (Nor).
L 10·8 cm. Trond 862b.

497 **Oval brooch,** bronze. Lisbjerg (Den).
L 9·1 cm. Cop I C11331.

498 **Key pendant,** bronze. Ihre (Swe).
L 10·1 c. SHM 22917:183:1.

499 **Openwork purse mount,** bronze. Othem (Swe).
D 6·7 cm. SHM 11887:1.

500 **Four bridle mounts,** gilt-bronze. Borre (Nor).
Max. L 5·4 cm. Oslo C1804.

501 **Nine strap mounts,** bronze and gilt-bronze. Gokstad (Nor).
Max. L 5·3 cm. Oslo.

502 **Necklace and pendants,** gold and glass. Hon (Nor). Oslo C747–9.

503 **Disc brooch,** silver. Gotland (Swe).
D 7·8 cm. BM MLA 1901,7–18,1.

504 **Quatrefoil brooch and chain,** gilt-silver. Rinkaby (Swe).
L 27·5 cm. SHM 4578.

505 **Disc brooch,** silver. Nonnebakken (Den).
D 6·3 cm. Cop I C6271.

506 **Patrice,** bronze. Mammen (Den).
H 6·3 cm. Cop I C1067.

507 **Disc brooch,** silver. Tråen (Nor).
D 7·3 cm. Oslo 21858a.

508 **Horse harness-bow,** gilt-bronze and modern wood. Mammen (Den).
L 42·0 cm. Cop I C1063.

509 **Nine pendants,** gilt-bronze and silver. Vårby (Swe).
Max. H 4·6 cm. SHM 4516.

510 **Disc brooch,** gilt-silver. Hønsi (Nor).
D 3·2 cm. Ber 709.

511 **Thistle brooch terminal,** silver. Skaill (Sco).
L 8·6 cm. Ed IL 5.

512 **Cylindrical sleeve,** bone. Årnes (Nor).
H 6 cm. Trond 18308.

513 **Cylindrical sleeve,** bone. St Martin's le Grand (Eng).
H 4·7 cm. Museum of London.

514 **Button,** bone. London (Eng).
D 5·8 cm. BM MLA 66,2–24,1.

515 **Sword mount,** elk antler. Sigtuna (Swe).
W 10·1 cm. Sigtuna 1965.

516 **Disc brooch,** silver. Åspinge (Swe).
D 5 cm. SHM 6620:2.

517 **Disc brooch,** silver. Gerete (Swe).
D 5·9 cm. SHM 1219.

518 **Bird-shaped brooch,** gilt-silver. Gresli (Nor).
W 4·8 cm. Trond 2042.

519 **Weather-vane,** gilt-bronze. Söderala (Swe).
L 37·7 cm. SHM 16023.

520 **Crucifix,** silver. Trondheim (Nor).
L 11 cm. Trond 16978b.

521 **Armlet,** gilt-silver and niello. Undrom (Swe).
D 7·1 cm. SHM 1318.

522 **Terminal,** bronze. Gotland (Swe).
W 2·4 cm. SHM Med Dep 12194.

523 **Brooch,** silver. Tröllaskogur (Ice).
H 4 cm. Reyk 6524.

524 **Brooch,** silver. Lindholm Høje (Den).
W 3·2 cm. Aalborg 129x 1397.

525 **Disc brooch,** gilt-bronze. Pitney (Eng).
D 3·9 cm. BM MLA 1979, 11–1, 1.

526 **Mount,** bronze. Lincoln (Eng).
L 6·1 cm. Lincoln Arch. Trust DT741.SZ.AE108.

527 **Bowl,** silver. Lilla Valla (Swe).
D 16·5 cm. SHM 3099.

SECTION 11
Christianity

528 **Two panels,** wood. Flatatunga (Ice).
L 73·8 cm. Reyk 15296a and b.

529 **Crucifix,** silver. Birka grave 660 (Swe).
H 3·4 cm. SHM.

530 **Crucifix,** silver. Äspinge (Swe).
H 5·8 cm. SHM 6620:1.

531 **Crucifix,** silver. Trondheim (Nor).
L 8·5 cm. Trond 16978a.

532 **Crucifix,** silver. Lilla Klintegårda (Swe).
H 8·2 cm. SHM 980.

533 **Reliquary cross and chain,** silver. Gåtebo (Swe).
W 6·2 cm. SHM Med Dep 100.

534 **Cross,** silver. Birka grave 480 (Swe).
L 3·1 cm. SHM.

535 **Disc brooch,** gilt-bronze. Hedeby (Ger).
D 2·7 cm. Sch.

536 **Tau cross,** bronze. Thingvellir (Ice).
W 8·6 cm. Reyk 15776.

537 **Pencase lid,** wood. Lund (Swe).
L 33·3 cm. Kult 53436:1125.

538 **Gravestone.** St Pauls Churchyard (Eng).
L 57·5 cm. Museum of London.

539 **Book mount,** bronze. Holycross (Ire).
H 8·7 cm. Dub P.1053.

540 **Trial-piece,** bone. Dublin (Ire).
L 12·9 cm Dub E71:5706.

541 **Shrine of St Senan's bell,** bronze. Scattery Island (Ire).
H 12·2 cm. Dub 1919.1.

542 **Bell shrine of St Cuileann,** iron, bronze, silver and enamel. Ireland.
H 31·5 cm. BM MLA 89,9–2,22.

543 **Shrine of St Manchan,** bronze and wood. Ireland.
H c. 45 cm. Boher, private possession.

Major wooden replicas

Faering replica Gokstad (Nor). Århus.

Sledge replica Oseberg (Nor). Århus.

Wagon replica Oseberg (Nor). Århus.

Portal replica Urnes (Nor). Ber.